TRUTH: *Four Stories I Am Finally Old Enough to Tell*

Also by Ellen Douglas

TRUTH: *Four Stories I Am Finally Old Enough to Tell*

by ELLEN DOUGLAS

ALGONQUIN BOOKS
OF CHAPEL HILL
1998

Published by
ALGONQUIN BOOKS OF CHAPEL HILL
Post Office Box 2225
Chapel Hill, North Carolina 27515-2225

a division of
Workman Publishing
708 Broadway
New York, New York 10003

Library of Congress Cataloging-in-Publication Data
Douglas, Ellen, 1921–
    Truth : four stories I am finally old enough to tell /
  by Ellen Douglas.
       p.   cm.
     ISBN 1-56512-214-3
     1. Douglas, Ellen, 1921– —Biography.   2. Authors,
  American—20th century—Biography.   I. Title.
  PS3554.O825Z475   1998
  813'.54—dc21
  [B]   98-7238
                                                  CIP

10 9 8 7 6 5 4 3 2
First Edition

In memory of Gold Smith Sr.
and Gold Smith Jr.

"Forgetting is just another kind of remembering."

—Robert Penn Warren, *Brother to Dragons*

Acknowledgments

My thanks to the staff of the Mississippi Department of Archives and History for excerpts from the Lizzie McFarland Blakemore Collection and to the Mississippi Historical Society for excerpts from *Life, Letters and Papers of William Dunbar,* compiled by Eron Rowland. Thanks also to the Hill Library at Louisiana State University for excerpts from the Lemuel P. Conner and Family Papers and the William J. Minor and Family Papers, Louisiana and Lower Mississippi Valley Collections, LSU Libraries, Louisiana State University, Baton Rouge.

Thanks to Winthrop Jordan for reading and commenting on "On Second Creek," not to mention writing the book *Tumult and Silence at Second Creek,* which set me on a quest; to friends and family who have patiently read and listened to and commented on these tales; to Kathie Blankenstein, Tom Gandy, and Alma Carpenter for generously sharing their difficult kinds of expertise; and particularly to Gold Smith's widow and his friends who spoke to me about his life.

Contents

TRUTH: *Four Stories I Am Finally Old Enough to Tell*

GRANT

We are *forever* cleaning up our act.

—Robert Stone, "The Reason for Stories"

*T*HIS IS A STORY that has been waiting for me —and now I am old enough to tell it. Not that I had forgotten. How could I forget what happened in my house, under my nose, to me? I even thought from time to time about telling one of the stories that lay next to it, so to speak. There were the bees the night Grant died. There was Rosalie, who sat by him every day when he was dying, beautiful Rosalie, who had five children and sometimes came to work with a cut lip, a battered nose, a bruised temple. There were the day walks, the night walks. But I didn't want to tell those stories. Nothing came of thinking about them.

My husband's uncle came to live with us during the last year of his life. He was eighty-two. His wife had died several years earlier and he had no children. He had cancer.

He could have gone to a veterans' hospital—he was an Annapolis graduate, a retired naval officer. And there were other possibilities. Once he was too feeble to look after himself, he could have hired live-in help or gone into a nursing home. But we invited, insisted, and he came.

I knew him as one knows uncles-in-law who live in the same town—as a genial enough fellow who brought his fiddle to family Thanksgiving gatherings and played badly to my husband's piano accompaniment. I can see him now on those occasions, fiddle tucked under his chin, standing over the piano, stooping to read the music, an expression of deep but clearly ironic concentration on his face, his head bent, light bouncing off the balding scalp. They'd play easy pieces from a collection of violin and piano duets: "None but the Lonely Heart," "Humoresque," a Schubert serenade. After they finished a piece he'd sit down, lay the violin across his lap, and smile. "I always have trouble with the triplets in that one," he might say. And his mother, nearly ninety then and nodding in her wheelchair: "Grant plays so well. It's a pity his violin squeaks."

That was a family joke.

So . . . Why did we invite him in? Well, again, family

—he was family. One couldn't send him off to a veterans' hospital or put him in a home, could one? But I'm misstating the case. No one could send him anywhere. He was perfectly capable of sending himself anywhere he wished, or of staying where he was, in the house his wife had left to her own niece and nephew.

Now there's another story. His wife, Kathleen, who was fifteen years younger than he, had died suddenly of a stroke. She'd doubtless always believed he would die first (he'd been retired early from the navy after a coronary) and had consequently left him nothing. The house and what other modest property they had was in her name. His name was not even mentioned in her will.

Grant could have contested it, of course: in our state you can't leave all your property away from a spouse. But he would never have done such a dishonorable thing. In her will she had said what she wanted. It would be done.

In their dealings with him the niece and nephew were correct, but they were a cold pair to my way of thinking. Or maybe it's just that they were like me, had other things to think about besides aged uncles-in-law. They gave him permission to live in the house for the rest of his life. So that there would be no confusion about the title, they paid the taxes and he reimbursed them. They didn't charge him any rent. He paid repairs and upkeep.

Now I ask you, no matter how much younger you were than your husband, no matter if he'd had a coronary, would you leave everything away from him? Wouldn't you think he might by chance survive you? You might get run over by a truck or stung to death by hornets or drown or get trapped in a burning house, or God knows what. Surely you would mention in your will the name of your husband of forty years.

The only light he shed on this story came when he moved in with us and was clearing out of her house the things that belonged to him. He brought with him his clothes, a couple of canvas-covered wicker trunks from his tour in the Philippines before the First World War, a beautiful Japanese tea set, some brass trays from India, a huge piece of tapa cloth, his easy chair. Everything else—the furniture, his wedding silver, china, linens, even the lovely carved cherry bed he'd had made for them by a local cabinetmaker—"All that stuff," he said, "I got it for her. It was hers. She left everything to them. So . . ."

He brought his navy dress uniform and his cocked hat, circa 1911. They're still in a closet somewhere in our house, the uniform in a mothproof bag, the hat stored in its leather case.

His sword he had given some years earlier to one of our sons. His violin he gave to my husband.

I think of one ray of light his wife shed on their marriage, although, I don't know, it may be misleading.

She was one of those large, soft-looking women, fair haired and blue eyed, who, statistical studies indicate, are most vulnerable in middle age to gall bladder attacks and diverticulitis. And indeed she did have the latter, although not for long, since she died when she was sixty.

In any case, what she said surprised me. She'd always seemed an easygoing, lively lady, ready for a good time, and I would have thought her tolerant of other people's foibles and failures and moral lapses. Not so, or not everybody's. We were talking of a man in the county who had left his wife for a woman who was widely known to have had in the course of her life a number of open love affairs—not so common among the small-town gentry of a couple of generations ago. I mean, people had *clandestine* affairs, of course, but not open ones. "She's filth," Grant's wife said to me when I commented once on this lady's charm and wit. "Filth. That's what they both are." She shivered and looked straight at me. (This was when I was quite a young woman, still focused almost to the exclusion of everything else on those lovely nights in bed.) "Men," she said. "There's only one thing men want and she gives it to them."

So, as you see, there's the story of their marriage, if one could dredge it up. And then . . . There's Rosalie.

But I think, instead, of the day Grant gave his sword to our second son. This was after his wife's death, but long before he came to live with us. As I've said, he had no sons of his own and my husband was the only child of his brother. There were no children of his blood except ours. He came walking slowly up the driveway the afternoon of our son's tenth birthday, bearing the sword in its leather scabbard with the gold tassel attached at the hilt. He didn't have a particularly soldierly bearing, looked more like a slightly seedy, gentle-mannered farmer than a potential admiral. Ross, our son, and three or four of his friends were sitting around a trestle table eating ice cream. Ross had been alerted ahead of time that his great-uncle intended to give him his sword and we had explained that this was a significant gift and he should feel honored. He stood up very straight and looked solemn and said thank you, but it was clear to me he was unimpressed—didn't quite know what use this sword, almost as tall as he was, would be to him. He and his friends were organizing a war with another neighborhood gang for the next day. Mud balls and BB guns would be their weapons of choice. We invited Grant in and he sat and had a drink with us. He was always convivial, happy to join you in a drink, never at a loss for words, often the butt of his own jokes.

So he came to live with us the last year of his life. He had refused treatment for the cancer. "I'm too old to let somebody cut on me," he'd said. "It's out of the question." He knew that he probably had less than a year to live.

The first few months he used to take a long walk every morning through the humming, buzzing late-spring world, bees swarming around the honeysuckle vines on the back fence, towhees calling, flickers drilling for bugs in the bark of the pecan tree, squirrels chasing each other up and down the trunk. He'd walk slowly, head a little forward, determined to go as far as he could; and then he'd return even more slowly, going to his room by the side door into the wing. He'd stop there sometimes and watch the squirrels. One day he pointed out to me that a wren had built her nest in the potted fern by the side door.

I never joined him on these walks. I didn't have time.

In the afternoon one of his friends or his brother might come to sit with him for a while; at night he and our youngest son sometimes played bridge with my husband and me. Grant was a good bridge player— indifferent, though, whether he won or lost. Or, some nights, he'd go back to his room and watch TV.

Later, as he grew weaker, he walked up and down our front sidewalk every day, too feeble to risk getting far from the house. Then he began to walk at night, up and down the long hall that led from the main part of our house past the two bedrooms where our sons were asleep, to his room and bath at the very back of the wing.

I still slept lightly, a habit most women keep after the years when the least sound from a child's room will wake you, and of course I heard Grant tramping up and down the hall. The first time, I got up and went back to see what was the matter. He was in his bathrobe, his sparse gray hair disheveled, his face drawn. For the first time I noticed how thin he'd gotten.

"What's the matter, Grant?" I asked.

"I'm getting a little exercise," he said. He gave me the same look of ironic concentration I'd seen on his face when he was playing the violin, as if to say, *I don't expect you to think I'm any good, but I'll give it a try.* This time it was, *I don't expect you to believe me, but act as if you do.*

Or was that what his look said? Might there have been a question in his eyes? An invitation to join him? Or was it deep knowledge of my fears, my self-absorption?

I knew he was in pain. He wasn't walking up and down the hall for exercise. I said to myself that I didn't want to invade his privacy and went back to bed. Next day I called the doctor and told him Grant needed something stronger—morphine, Dilaudid—and he called in a new prescription. For some weeks Grant continued to walk every night. I would hear him and put my pillow over my head.

It was during this period or a few weeks later that Grant hired Rosalie. She had worked for him and his wife a couple of days a week for several years, and then, after his wife died, had cooked for him. She was a splendid cook and the kind of woman who could take charge of a household—intelligent and aggressive. She could have been an office manager or a clothes buyer in a department store (she had a flair for style) or perhaps a lawyer (she knew how to get what she wanted from almost anyone). Unfortunately none of these careers had been open to her. She was an illiterate black woman and the year was 1964.

When Grant had moved in with us, he'd given Rosalie a month's severance and a bonus and recommended her to several friends. She'd had no trouble getting another job. Then, when he began to weaken, could no longer trust himself alone in the bathroom, and needed help with dressing, he arranged with the family for whom she worked to share her time. She came every morning for a couple of hours, helped him with his bath, made his bed, and, if he wished, fixed a cold supper and left it for him in the refrigerator.

Sometimes she would stay for a while after he was bathed and dressed and comfortable. She was a talker, loved to visit—and so did he. He may already have been talking to her about dying. Or maybe she began it. She was a devout Christian, offered up a marvelous strong soprano voice to God every week at church and was president of the choir.

In any case during those morning visits he began to teach her to read, using the Bible as his text. Oh, how deeply Rosalie wanted to learn to read the Bible —more, I think, than wanting the changes that reading might make in her life. It was reading the Bible, I'm sure of it, that she was focused on. She needed it, needed the support of religion, I mean. She was trapped in her life, not just because she couldn't read, but because she had five children and an abusive husband whom she couldn't leave as long as he paid the rent and made a contribution to the household expenses.

And Grant was bored, of course.

So he occupied himself teaching her. Some days I'd go back and find them sitting side by side, him in his easy chair, Rosalie with a straight-backed desk chair drawn close to his. Together they leaned over his battered King James Bible, turned the onionskin pages. It must have been easier for her to begin to pick out words because she knew so much of it by heart. He'd move his finger along a line: "'I sink in deep mire, where there is no standing: I—am—come—into—deep—waters—where—the floods—overflow—me.'" Or: "'Bless the Lord, oh my soul; and all that is within me, bless his holy name.'" She could read that easily or pretend to, moving her finger from word to word once he started her with "Bless." "Look at every word," he'd say, and they'd do it again. "'B-b-bless—Bless the Lord —oh—my—soul.'"

One day, putting away clothes in my son's room, I heard him laughing and then Rosalie, raising her voice, "Now you know that ain't it, Mr. Grant." I stopped to listen.

"But there it is," he said, "and you ought to like it. 'I am black, but comely, O ye daughters of Jerusalem,' and 'I am the rose of Sharon, and the lily of the valleys.' And how about this: 'Stay me with flagons, Comfort me with apples: for I am sick of love.' That's the bride talking."

"Oh, Mr. Grant," she said, "that's talking about Jesus and the church. The church is the bride of Jesus. That's not about what you're talking about."

He laughed again. "Anyhow," he said. "It's poetry. It's beautiful poetry."

"It's the Word of God," Rosalie said.

I tiptoed away.

I don't want to wander here. I want to stick with the long, agonizing last months of Grant's illness. Still, I have to tell you before I go on how beautiful Rosalie was. It would be commonplace to compare her profile to Nefertiti's and, remembering her—the full lips, the heavy-lidded eyes and slightly flattened nose—I think she's more like those elegant attendant ladies on the wall of one of the Ramses' tombs. But there was nothing stiff or narrow or Egyptian about her body. You admired her face when she walked in, and then, when she swung a strong, round hip against the kitchen door to bump it shut, you'd begin to wish your waist was as supple, your legs as shapely, your breasts as softly ample as hers. What a pleasure to have such a person to look at every day.

But one day she would come to work sullen, turning her face away, an eyelid darkened, not with kohl but with the greenish purple stain of a bruise, her sensuous lips cut where her husband's fist had crushed them against her teeth. She'd threaten to leave him or to swear out a restraining order against him and for a while everything would be quiet.

As the weeks passed, it became more and more difficult for me to walk down the long back hall in our house, to raise my hand and knock on Grant's door, to hear his breathy voice saying, "Come in," to listen to his labored breathing, look into his gaunt face.

There he was, a huge presence in our house, and he was family; but I didn't want to see him or to think about him. Every day, morning and afternoon, I forced myself to go back to his room and stay for at least ten minutes. I felt the weight of my watch on my wrist and willed myself not to look at it, but I knew to the minute when I could leave.

During this period several of his friends abandoned him. At first their visits would be less frequent—once a week, once every two weeks. Then they stopped coming altogether. If I saw one of them in the grocery store or in the post office picking up mail, he'd inquire for Grant and say, "I've been out of town." Or, "He's so weak, I don't want to disturb him. But give him our love."

"Yes," I'd say. "All right. I will."

His brother, my father-in-law, still, and to the end, came every day.

There can be only one reason why I hated so deeply the ordeal of going back to visit with this lovely old man. He was dying. His dying was a terrible disgrace, an embarrassment not to be endured. That's the story I could not tell. I abandoned him, too.

In the middle of it, I didn't know I was abandoning

him, did I? I was busy. I had three children. I had my own work to do, my obligations. And I needed to go fishing, to see my parents, to go out with my friends, to lie beside my husband in our warm bed.

The town where we lived was on a cutoff bend of the Mississippi River, a man-made lake, long and still on windless summer days between its confining levees, fringed with willows and cypress and cottonwood trees, jumping with bream and bass and crappie and catfish. When they were younger, the children and I had picnicked and fished and skied and swum its waters. Now that the eldest was in college and the two younger in high school, they were not interested in picnics with Mama, but I still needed, as I always had, to be out on the water, to hear waves lapping the green sides of my fishing boat, to lie on the sandbar with my friends and watch the sun go down behind the cottonwood trees. I was busy, caught up in my life.

It sometimes seemed to me in those days, as I told a friend when we were out on the lake together, as if our house were panting, the walls swelling and shrinking, as if it were breathing sex. I'd hear the boys come in on weekend nights, would pretend not to hear the soft voices of the girls they sometimes brought with them. In the kitchen, in the morning, I would hear Rosalie teasing them about their girlfriends, asking about this one or that one. And at night, when they came in from a party, from skinny-dipping off the sandbar, from lying on the levee with the radio on ... What can I say to tell you how alive that household was?

One night, Ross came in at two or three in the morning, disheveled and half-buttoned, lipstick smeared across his cheek, and found Grant sitting on the floor in the hall, conscious, but unable to get up. Half-asleep, I heard them talking to each other and tiptoed out to see what was the matter. Ross was standing over Grant, buttoning his shirt. "Well ... ," he was saying.

And Grant was laughing. "I was waiting for you," he said. "I knew you'd get here eventually. But look at you!" And then, "Don't try to pick me up. Don't pull on me. I might come apart."

I stood appalled. Ross should not have to face this.

But he stooped without a word—strong as a stevedore he was in those days—and slipped one arm under Grant's shoulders, the other under his knees, lifted him, as it appeared, without effort, and carried him back to his room. I heard them laughing together, waited a minute, then pretended I had just gotten up, walked back to Grant's room, stuck my head in, and asked if I could help.

"No, no," Grant said. "We're OK."

It was shortly after this that he said he needed someone with him at night, and from then on he had round-the-clock sitters, Rosalie in the morning and two other women who came in from three until eleven and eleven until seven.

One morning during those last weeks, not so long before he lapsed into a coma, just as I raised my hand to knock at his door, I heard him say to Rosalie in a measured, thoughtful way, "Yes. Yes." A pause, and then, "I do. I do. I don't try to know what it'll be like, but I know I'll see Kathleen."

Rosalie said Amen.

"But what will *see* mean?" he said. "I don't know. Somehow she and I will be . . ." Again a thoughtful pause. "She will be there with me."

"Yes, Lord," Rosalie said. "Amen, Mr. Grant."

He did not speak of those things with me.

There is one more thing about Rosalie and Grant. I had thought I could leave it out, but I find that I can't. It happened after he was entirely bedridden, after everything had to be done for him.

I realize now it's usually the case that one hires men to take care of male patients, but curiously enough I didn't think about that at the time and apparently neither did Grant. We'd started with Rosalie and it seemed natural to keep on with her, and then to find two other women, one a cousin of hers who came with a string of recommendations, the other a trained LPN.

In any case, I came into the kitchen one morning from the car, bringing bags of groceries, and found Rosalie standing, her back to me, at the sink.

"Morning, Rosalie," I said, and turned to go out for another load.

"I got to leave," she said. "I can't nurse him any more."

"What?" I stood in the doorway staring at her. "What's the matter?"

"He wants me to touch him," she said.

"Rosalie!"

"He wants me to touch him."

Grant was already at the stage where he spent much of the day dozing, drifted in and out of sleep. Last time the doctor had come to see him, I'd gone back to his room and stood by to make sure we were doing everything we should. The doctor had touched his arm, raised it and lowered it, helped him sit up, pressed the soles of his feet, tapped his knees. Afterwards, as we walked to the car, he'd said, "It's in his brain now. I don't think it will be long. I'm increasing the morphine. We don't want him to suffer."

"He wants me to touch him," Rosalie said. "I can't see after him any more."

"Oh, Rosalie, Rosalie."

She was weeping. I put my arms around her, patted her shoulder distractedly. "It's in his brain," I said. "The cancer. And the pain medicine. He doesn't know what he's saying."

"I'm scared of him," she said. "I don't want no part of that."

"Rosalie, he's so weak, he couldn't possibly hurt you," I said.

"He says, 'Come on, help me. Let's see if I can get it up.' And then he laughed. I got to go," she said.

But of course she didn't. She stayed to the end.

And I was going to leave out the bees, too. The bees seemed, to begin with, no more than a bizarre detail of what happened the night Grant died.

It was toward four o'clock in the morning when the night nurse came to our bedroom door and roused my husband and me. "Mr. Grant has passed," she said.

We got up, put on bathrobes, tiptoed, so as not to wake the boys, down the long hall to his room. He had been unconscious for many days. His body, under the sheet and light blanket, was barely an outline, thin to emaciation, his cheeks sunken. But he seemed now no less alive than when I'd looked in on him the day before. He was still himself, the lines that his life had made still vivid in his flesh, his dignity untouched. I even seemed to see that ironic half-smile on his face: *Well, I'll give it a try then.*

I laid my hand on his chest, feeling for a heartbeat, thinking the sitter must be mistaken, put my fingers on his lips to catch a breath. But Grant was dead, as she knew quite well. She had already cleaned him up after the sphincter relaxed; had changed his pajamas before she called us; had opened the curtains and the windows to air out the room and turned on all the lights in the hall. She had even opened the outside door to the mild spring night. She knew her job.

Now she said that she had done all she needed to do and, if we were agreeable, she would go on home.

"All right," my husband said. "Certainly." And he walked with her to the door, thanking her, saying he'd call her in the morning, put her check in the mail, let her know about funeral arrangements. She'd told us that she was a nurse who always attended her patients' funerals. "I show respect," she'd said.

It was at the door, when she couldn't go out, that we saw the bees.

The bees, part of the colony that lived in a high hollow in the pecan tree in the side yard, were swarming. How could such a thing be? Swarming in the middle of the night? But there they were, a heaving mass of them clustered on the screen door, sheets of them clinging to the window screens in the long hall. My husband saw the nurse out through the front door and came back. What should we do?

"If we turn off the lights," he said, "maybe they'll decide to move. They can't start a new hive on a screen door."

So we turned the lights off and groped our way to our bedroom, sat down, stared at each other. What do you do at four o'clock in the morning with your dead uncle cooling toward rigor in his bed and a swarm of bees on the door?

After a while my husband said, "I should call Daddy."

"It's too early," I said. "Let's wait until six o'clock. He's usually up by six."

"The doctor," he said. "The death certificate. We forgot. And maybe we should call the funeral home to come and get him. I mean, before the boys wake up."

"Yes," I said. "I think we should."

"But what about the bees? How will they get him out the door?"

We went back to check. The bees were still there.

And then we found ourselves outside with burning spills of newspaper flaring in the darkness. We would smoke them into docility and then brush them away so the undertaker could come in with his gurney. But the bees clung and buzzed and crawled over each other and stayed.

We called the doctor and then the funeral home. Of course they managed well enough, rolling the gurney out the long way, down the hall, across the living room, negotiating the sharp turn into the entrance hall, and out the front door.

He was gone.

By then it was almost six o'clock and we called my husband's father. The sun was up. The wren was calling from the fern by Grant's door, where she'd made her nest. While we were in the kitchen making coffee, talking about arrangements, about whom we needed to call, who would be pallbearers, the bees must have decided to leave. They were gone when we went back to the wing to wake the boys.

It was Rosalie who told us why they'd swarmed.

"That fool should've known," she said, talking about the night nurse. "Any fool ought to know. You got to tell the bees immediately when somebody dies." But then she thought better of what she'd said. "Maybe she didn't know there were bees up in that tree," she said. "I saw them, but there wasn't any reason for her to have noticed. She don't come on 'til eleven. How she's going to see bees going in and out in the middle of the night?"

"But what do you mean, Rosalie?" I said. "Why do you have to tell the bees when somebody dies?"

"I forget y'all are not from the country," she said. "In the country they say you got to tell the bees or they'll swarm, they'll leave the hive. I don't s'pose it makes no difference whether it's a hive or a tree. You got to go out right away and say, 'The master is dead,' and then, maybe, something like, 'I'm the new master,' so they'll know somebody is in charge or . . . I don't know."

I sat down at the kitchen table and put my head in my hands and she sat down across from me. We looked at each other and wept.

About Rosalie. Soon after Grant's death she began to go to night school, leaving her fifteen-year-old to look after the younger kids. She got her high school equivalency diploma; and then she got a much better job and she left her wicked husband for a while, although I've heard that every now and then she went back to him. At least she was freer, able to leave him if she liked.

And, as it turns out, the will, Rosalie, the bees, all those tales, are a part of the story I didn't tell when Grant died. Now, twenty-odd years later, I can tell that story. Death has become, so to speak, family.

Sometimes, in the morning, when the bees are just

beginning to stir (I wake early these days, as old people so often do), I fill my coffee cup and stand listening in the kitchen. The boys are long gone now on their separate ways; the house is still, no longer breathing and swelling with their energy. I take my cup then and go out into the yard and listen to the raucous cries of the jay, the flicker's jackhammer drill, the *tchk, tchk* of the squirrels chasing each other through the high branches of the pecan tree. The wind lifts the leaves and there at a fork I see the dark hole where years ago a limb was torn away in a storm and where now the bees still make their home. They've filled the hole with comb, and comb hangs down against the tree trunk. Singly, the bees drift out, circle, drop downward, and begin to draw nectar from the daffodils, to pollinate the clover on the ditch bank, to tumble like drunken bawds in the deep, intoxicating magnolia cups. I lay my hand against the bark and tell the bees that I, too, will die. I admonish them not to swarm, not to leave us, but to stay in their hollow in the pecan tree, to keep making for us all their golden, fragrant, dark, sweet honey.

JULIA AND NELLIE

Heaven and earth have sworn that the truth shall remain forever hidden.

—Isaac Bashevis Singer, "The Dead Fiddler"

TO AVOID CONFUSION, I must tell you that, although this "true" story will begin with an account, by a real person, Adah Williams of Greenville, Mississippi, of the surreptitious blessing of a grave on a farm called The Forest in Adams County, Mississippi, Miss Adah will vanish from my story. Don't wait for her to reappear. Her presence, although essential to the story, is accidental. She would never have spoken to me of Dunbar Marshall's grave if we hadn't happened to spend two hours together one day in 1948, driving south from Greenville along Highway 61. But it was her curious tale that set me wondering and asking questions about certain lives lived out in obscurity a long time ago.

It's her account of the blessing of the grave that I recall most vividly; but entangled with that memory are tag ends of information that I may have acquired then or some other time from someone else—fleeting memories of people I knew as a child, questions I asked years later that were answered or left unanswered, whole scenes that have mysteriously stayed with me. Of the people involved, only two were still alive at that time and they were very old. Now, of course, all are dead. That's why I put *true* in quotation marks. I can't honestly say I am telling the truth—not for sure—and there is no one left to correct me if I'm wrong.

But I know, or think I know, that Mr. Marshall lived for a while at Longwood (another house near Natchez), and that he died at The Forest. One objective, verifiable fact is that he has a gravestone dedicated to him by his wife, Fanny, in the Forest cemetery. Presumably he's under it.

Before you hear Miss Adah's story, let me tell you about Natchez and Longwood and The Forest. Think first, not of Tara and hoopskirts and ruthless Southern belles, but rather of churches, bells ringing for Sunday services and Wednesday night prayer meeting, of ladies and gentlemen and children in worn but respectable Sunday clothes gathering to worship God and to find some order and joy in a difficult world. Think, too, of early-twentieth-century poverty, of making do in a depression that began in the riverine South with—what?

The end of the Civil War? The advent of railroads and the loss of the river as a highway? The feckless clear-cutting of that hilly land? The coming of the boll weevil in 1915? All of these. Sixty-odd years ago when I was growing up, everyone I knew went to church and almost everyone was poor. Not hungry. Not in rags (only the Negroes were in rags), but poor.

To me ours was never a doomish, a threatening poverty, but rather the comfortable limitations that may seem to a child to be—and be, at least for a while—security. In those days paint curled off my grandmothers' ceilings. Drapes had not been replaced in years. Scraps of newspaper folded into spills stood in a jar on the mantelpiece for use as matches to light my aunt's cigarettes from the fire glowing in the coal grate. (Surely there was money for matches, wasn't there, if there was money for cigarettes? Or was the jar of spills evidence of Presbyterian thrift carried to its limits?) In any event, for us children, there were books (mostly very old ones, it's true) and someone always ready to read or tell you a story. And in the country there were lakes to swim in, creeks to wade, ponds with ducks to be fed, and woods to explore.

Here, on the outskirts of the small town of Natchez, is Longwood—a wildly extravagant Moorish castle of a mansion (Nutt's Folly, people called it) left unfinished in

1861 when the Civil War broke out. No one in the Nutt family ever again had the money (or perhaps the hubris, either) to finish it. Instead, they and subsequent descendants sold away or lost most of the land, lived on the finished ground floor, and left the top four floors (still littered with scaffolding, dried-up buckets of paint, canvas carpenters' aprons, ladders, and tools) to mice and owls and bats and children's explorations. I remember as a child climbing among the rafters and floor joists and looking out from the windowed dome over abandoned fields and shaggy lawns, over thickets of gum and locust and pecan that I knew must once have been gardens, because in their seasons I could see unkillable spirea and daffodils and crepe myrtles still blooming.

Here, too, is The Forest, another country place we occasionally visited — no more doomish or gloomish than Longwood. The main house — built by an ancestor named William Dunbar — had burned years before the Civil War, and the old carriage house had been converted into a long low cottage with a gallery across the front (as I seem to recall, although I haven't been there in more than fifty years). There, in the 1930s, my great-aunt Marian Davis lived with her husband, Jamie, whom she'd married in late middle age.

I remember we especially liked going to The Forest because Jamie and Marian had a donkey they would let us ride. Hard now to think of anything less exciting—I can't remember ever being able to kick that passive beast into a trot. But ride we did. The donkey existed. My sister has a snapshot of the two of us and a cousin all sitting on him, our feet almost touching the ground. And then, when we tired of riding, while the grown-ups sat on the gallery in quiet and intimate conversation, we'd explore the ruin of the old house—nothing left but two or three crumbling columns and the half-buried foundation—and wander through the family graveyard close by.

The graveyard is the focus of Miss Adah's story.

We were driving south from Greenville, where we both lived, on a lush spring day in 1948, primroses and vetch awash along the ditch banks, bean and cotton rows whirling by, green spokes in the dark, flat disk of the Delta. Miss Adah, an elderly friend of my mother-in-law's, had caught a ride with me as far as Vicksburg, where she would visit cousins. I was going to Natchez to see my grandmothers, both in their late eighties, both lively still, but undeniably fragile, moving toward death. We'd been exchanging tales of mutual friends and family connections—as Southern women are still wont to do when they begin to get acquainted.

"Natchez isn't a real town, is it?" she said. "Faulkner might have invented it."

Miss Adah was one of those gracious, self-confident women who used to be the products of regular army families. She sorted people out: officers, noncoms, privates, and foreigners. She'd seen the world and could cope with it. And she'd married a wealthy Delta planter and no doubt could cope with him, too.

"Well," I said, "the landscape . . . The woods. The Spanish moss. All those movie-set pre–Civil War houses. But—I don't know—I see it differently. Longwood, for example. My father's family (he and his parents and his three brothers) lived at Longwood for a year or two when the boys were in high school. Before that, they lived too far out in the country to go to school and their mother taught them. But when they needed to learn geometry and trig and Latin to prepare for college, they rented the Longwood house. Near enough to town to ride their horses to school. Later, my grandfather inherited a little money and they bought a house in town."

"Lived there?" Miss Adah said. "At Longwood?"

"So in a way, for me," I went on, "there's nothing Faulknerian about it. I see that finished ground floor as a home, with my grandmother's furniture in it—the music box, the square piano, my grandmother's little desk, littered with bills and letters to answer, her brown wicker rocker drawn up to the coal grate, the Bible on her sewing table, just as I remember it in the house in town."

"But Miss Julia Nutt—Dr. Haller Nutt's daughter —she always lived at Longwood," Miss Adah said.

"No, I think—let's see—I think she lived there sometimes. But I know my father and his brothers . . . She must have been living somewhere else when she rented Longwood to my grandfather. I seem to recall that sometimes she lived at The Forest. Maybe that's where she was when . . ."

"But that's impossible," she said. "There was a madwoman living at The Forest. A madwoman named Davis."

"Oh?" I said. "But . . ."

"Yes. I suppose she's dead now," she said. "A countrywoman, I think—*plain*—but I'm not sure. Maybe from an old family."

I'd been about to say, "But that was probably later." Now, though, I felt myself closing down. I wouldn't volunteer any more of my own vaguely remembered family gossip. I'd listen instead, noncommittally, to what Miss Adah had to say about a madwoman named Davis, who was in fact my great-aunt, whom I knew well, and who in my view was not mad at all. Feisty, yes. Vigorous. Opinionated. But not mad.

"A patch over one eye. Fanny said she had a patch over one eye."

That was my great-aunt all right. She'd lost an eye to acute glaucoma in her early fifties.

"I suppose Miss Julia must have moved back to Longwood at some point," I said. "I don't know. It was all such a long time ago."

"Have you ever been out there?" Miss Adah said. "To The Forest, I mean."

"Yes. Mama and my grandmother used to take us out there sometimes when we were children."

"So then you know that old Mr. Dunbar Marshall (his wife, Fanny, was a distant cousin of mine) lived there for a while?"

I did in fact have a vague memory of having seen an old gentleman sitting on the gallery, of knowing who he was because I'd seen him elsewhere—where?

"He's buried in The Forest cemetery," she said.

"Oh?"

"I believe (family gossip—somebody heard it from Fanny) she was abroad when Dunbar died. They'd been separated for some years, but they were always on friendly terms. Of course," Miss Adah said, "they were both Catholic, so there was never any question of a divorce."

My impulse now is to recall that I said, "Like Spencer Tracy," just to be catty. But I don't think the Spencer Tracy–Katharine Hepburn affair was common knowledge as early as 1948. I don't know what I said or if I said anything. I was probably silent, watching the ribbon of highway ahead and the orderly bean and cotton rows spinning by, thinking of that graveyard—untended, if my memory of it was accurate, surrounded by a foot-thick, six-foot-high brick wall, with a wrought iron gate. I could hear the creak of the gate on its hinges when my sister and I struggled to push it open. Saplings had sprung up inside, and at one place the humped roots of a very old cherrybark oak were tilting a gravestone.

"In any case," Miss Adah said, "the story is that when Fanny got home, she went down to see about a stone for his grave. No one down there, I suppose, who would have been responsible for that. His immediate family were all dead. And there might not have been anybody with money to spare to pay for it, even if someone had wanted to. But Fanny had her own money —from her father's family. It was when she went to call on Dunbar's parish priest, to hear the details of the funeral, that she found out he'd been buried at The Forest, that . . ." A little shiver as of revulsion went over Miss Adah's shoulders. She too was Catholic, as I well knew. "No confession," she said. "No extreme unction. No mass. Not in consecrated ground."

"But why? . . ." I said. "Why not in the Natchez cemetery?"

"Well, I suppose they'd have had to buy a grave space there," she said. "And he was a Dunbar descendant, after all. He had a perfect right to be buried in the Dunbar cemetery. I suppose the Davis woman decided that was the cheapest place to bury him. As I said, none of his family was alive except for Fanny and she was in Europe—had been for years."

"Oh," I said, "I see," although I didn't.

"But what Fanny learned was that the burial service had been Presbyterian. No priest. No *nothing*."

"No nothing," I echoed, thinking to myself what Aunt Marian would say about calling a Presbyterian funeral *nothing*.

"Exactly. And when she went out to get permission to hold a memorial service, to bless the grave, she—the one-eyed lady—flew into a frenzy." Miss Adah broke off. "Do you know who she was?" she asked.

I was beginning to feel vaguely disloyal to my great-aunt. I didn't like hearing her called "the Davis woman," although I was perfectly sure she wouldn't give a damn what Miss Adah—or anyone else—thought of what she'd done with Mr. Dunbar Marshall's remains. It was just that my silence was beginning to seem sneaky. Besides, since Miss Adah had Natchez connections, the truth would come out. She'd learn exactly who I was.

"As a matter of fact," I said, "the Miss Davis you're talking about is my great-aunt. I seem to have a vague recollection of seeing Mr. Marshall—everybody called him Cousin Dunny—at The Forest. But I didn't know he was buried out there and I didn't know he had a wife. I never heard his funeral discussed. No reason why I should. He was just one of those people children see from time to time when they tag along with grown people."

One of those people, I was thinking, who die and disappear and whom you never hear mentioned again. And thinking, too, how lonely he must have been. No family. A Catholic among Presbyterians. No priest to hear his last confession.

"Mercy," Miss Adah said, "I hope I haven't offended you."

"No," I said. "I'm interested. After all, she does have a patch over her eye. And if she isn't a madwoman, she's certainly set in her ways."

"Well, I can't take it back, even if she's your aunt," Miss Adah said. "She flew into a frenzy. Told Fanny he'd had a perfectly good Presbyterian burial with a Presbyterian preacher and if that wasn't enough to get him into heaven, he'd just have to go the other way."

"Hmmm," I said. I could see Aunt M. running a hand through her short gray hair as if to make it stand on end, cocking her head on one side to favor a sharp, ferocious good eye, and saying (firmly if not frenziedly) to anything she disapproved of, "NO."

"Fanny was humiliated," Miss Adah said. "Not just humiliated. Undone."

"I can imagine," I murmured.

"But not defeated," Miss Adah said. "Not defeated. Naturally she went back to the priest for advice, and— I'm vague on this. I think . . . He may have tried to persuade your aunt. I remember now. But your aunt was adamant. Immovable."

"Catholics have never had much luck persuading Presbyterians, have they?" I said. "Or vice versa." I was thinking of Foxe's *Book of Martyrs* on the shelf in my father's secretary and of the note in my great-grandfather's family Bible regarding *his* grandfather, who "suffered much in the persecution of the church in the time of Mr. Erskine and Mr. Fisher's Secession."

"King Charles the First," Miss Adah said. "Wasn't it you people who turned him over to Cromwell?"

"I never understood that," I said. "He wasn't really Catholic, was he? Just Anglo-Catholic. Church of England. Couldn't he just as well have become a Presbyterian? And then it wouldn't have happened."

"Oh, he was a good Catholic, all right. He wanted the whole country to go back to the Church. And you turned him over to Cromwell. To be murdered! And what about St. Thomas More?"

"Not guilty," I said. "Henry the Eighth."

"Of course," she said. "I apologize."

"But then there's Bloody Mary," I said. "You all have your share of villains."

Yes. We were having this conversation about martyrs and persecutors in the year of our Lord 1948.

"It's a toss-up whose ancestors were more bloodthirsty," I said, but all she said was, "Hmmm."

After a minute she went on. "Anyhow Fanny took the priest and went out to The Forest. She thought they would just slip in quietly and bless the grave and depart without saying anything to your aunt. But the gate— the main gate—was locked. Padlocked. Chained."

I saw Aunt Marian again, slight but wiry, spikes of iron-gray hair fairly vibrating, mouth drawn down in a characteristically knowing half-smile, as she snapped the padlock through the links of chain.

The Forest cemetery now is just a few yards back from Interstate Highway 61, cheek by jowl with an oil field equipment storage area littered with piles of oil drums and rusting pipes, the huge carcasses of flatbed trailers, pumping units with square heads and long necks like strange prehistoric birds. There are cylindrical oil storage tanks large enough to live in. One pumping unit cranes its neck over the brick wall that in my childhood loomed above my head. The tall central cenotaph is dwarfed by an abandoned storage tank pocked with rust.

In the 1930s, though, there was no four-lane Highway 61. You came to The Forest on old 61, graveled by then, but once a dirt track between shale bluffs, worn deep into the crumbling earth, first by buffalo and the Natchez Indians, later by white settlers—by us. The scene Miss Adah described—Fanny and the priests coming back at night along that winding road, finding a place to conceal the cars while they did their work— has stuck in my mind for almost fifty years. For they did come back. Came toward midnight a couple of days later. It took Fanny that long to put the arrangements together. They came in two cars of the period (a Model A probably, if it belonged to the diocese, as it must have, and a Buick or a Cadillac, if Fanny was driving her own car). I can hear the loud *putt-putt* and rattle of the Model A, the smooth purr of the Cadillac. Fanny and two priests (Miss Adah said there were two priests), and a couple of acolytes. They followed the ancient road, turned off on a dirt track that Fanny had scouted out the day before with the help of two black men who lived on an adjoining place. They parked. No one would have seen them. Like the road, the track was sunk deep between its shale banks. And who, in any case, would have been driving down old 61 at midnight? There, deep in the night, they met the two black men with whom Fanny had made her arrangements. The men lit their torches (Flambeaux, Miss Adah called them. They were doubtless fat pine knots) and led the procession in, across a pasture at a point where the locust-post-and-barbed-wire fence was half down. All they had to do was push the leaning post lower and step across the strands of wire it had held in place. They entered the woods then, Miss Adah said, and made their way to the cemetery.

"Can't you picture it?" she said. "Imagine! The deep woods. Spanish moss hanging low. Torches flaming! Censers smoking . . ."

Really! I thought. *Really!*

They did whatever needed to be done to help Dunny begin his journey from hell through purgatory toward heaven and then they left. Later, doubtless, masses would be said for his soul. Candles would be lit. Money would change hands from time to time over the years.

"So now," Miss Adah said, with considerable satisfaction, it seemed to me, "a piece of the Dunbar cemetery is Catholic."

*I*t strikes me that there are going to be confusions and frustrations in this tale regarding kinship and identity. For those who, unlike most Southerners, black and white (and members of other clans, for that matter), are not used to keeping lists of relatives in their heads, I append here for ready reference a partial list of characters and a brief history of the two houses:

> Grandmother One—my maternal grandmother
> Marian Davis—her sister-in-law and my great-aunt
> Grandmother Two (Nellie)—my paternal grand-
>   mother
> John—husband of Grandmother Two
> Corinne—Nellie's sister
> Julia Nutt—Nellie's friend
> Dunbar Marshall, called Dunny—cousin to all these
>   people
> Fanny—Dunbar's wife

An abbreviated history of two planations near Natchez

LONGWOOD ("Nutt's Folly")	THE FOREST
(Of Moorish castle design, only the first floor completed.)	(Burned before the Civil War, leaving only the carriage house.)
Built in 1860–61 by Haller Nutt	Built in 1793 by William Dunbar

Came down by inheritance
   to Julia Nutt

(author's paternal grand-
   mother's best friend)

Came down in the
   family to Marian
   Davis and Dunbar
   Marshall

(relatives on author's
   mother's side)

I dropped Miss Adah off in Vicksburg that spring afternoon and drove on south to Natchez. Grandmother One was expecting me and I found her sitting on her front porch, as she often was on spring and summer afternoons, ready to pass the time of day with whoever happened to walk by. I couldn't wait to ask her about the midnight invasion of The Forest Cemetery.

"I don't believe it," she said. "I just don't believe it. *She* was the madwoman—Fanny. If Marian had known she was doing that, she'd . . . God knows what she'd have done."

My grandmother often said, "Oh, Lord" or "Lord knows," but "God"? Only when she was really talking about God.

"God knows," she said again. And then, "Of course we all knew she'd come down here. That she wanted the grave blessed or consecrated, or whatever they do. Marian told me at the time. And then, afterwards, later,

I knew she'd put a stone—a large slab covering the entire grave . . . Marian didn't object to that. Although . . . *Dedicated by his loving wife, Fanny?* It's clear what she meant to imply: You people buried him, but I had to come all the way back from Europe and buy a marker for his grave.

"But blessing—*consecrating*—the Dunbar cemetery? As if it needed it? And after forty years apart, with never a peep from her? Without the faintest indication that . . . Not, of course, that there was any reason for her to stay in touch with him."

She shook her head and was quiet for a while, pressing her lips together now and again, as very old people do, as if she were biting off an invisible thread.

Now, in 1948, her lids drooped heavily over milky, almost sightless eyes. But when she was young, I knew from her wedding photograph, her gaze had been skeptical, ironic, compelling a response. *Look at this ridiculous getup,* she seemed to say, gazing out of the picture. *What do you think of it?* Now, though, she saw only vague shapes, used her voice to draw you in. Sitting on her front porch, across the street from the cathedral, its red bulk rising from among squat live oak trees, she'd listen for a familiar step, recognize her passing neighbors by their voices, call them in for a chat.

But it was still true that nothing much escaped her.

Across the street a troop of children passed, followed by two sisters in their dark blue habits, carried along by the white sails of their wimples, rosaries swinging from their belts. She heard the marching steps. "Children going to mass?"

"I reckon so," I said.

"Who knows why they separated in the first place," she said. "Fanny and Dunbar. But whatever the reason, they were separated. Even if they were not divorced. And as for that, my dear, the Catholics didn't have a corner on staying married and making your own discreet arrangements. I'd be the first to admit that. Nobody got divorced in those days. But Fanny and Dunbar were totally separated, totally. Two years after they married—they lived the whole time abroad, spent months on a European tour, and then settled in Italy, so we heard—two years later he came back here without a word to anyone about what had gone wrong. Not a word that I ever heard . . ."

"But if he was not a Catholic . . ."

"Oh, I suppose he must have converted when he married her. There wouldn't have been the possibility of marriage otherwise, given her family." She shrugged. "As you know, conversion would never be a matter of convenience in *our* family, but it must have been for him. He certainly, as far as I know, never went to mass once he escaped their clutches. And then! For her to come back here after he died and! . . ."

"But why should Aunt Marian care what Fanny did?" I said. "What difference did it make?"

"Ah, that's a puzzle, isn't it? Why? What difference did it make? Certainly it wasn't personal. Marian wasn't even living at The Forest when Dunny died, was she? Julia was in charge. She made the arrangements. But, regardless of that, for Fanny to come back — to *imply* . . . As if Dunny had wanted confession and a Catholic burial, as if he'd called out for a priest when he was dying. You see? Fanny, after forty years of living a life of ease in Florence — yes, Italy. She stayed on after he came home, spent her life abroad . . ."

"But why Miss Julia Nutt?" I said. "Why was she in charge? What was her connection with Mr. Marshall?"

"And how long had he been dead? At least a couple of years. Ridiculous! Did they think God had been hanging around waiting for the grave to be blessed before he could decide what to do with Dunny?" Grandmother laughed and shook her head. "Not that I have anything against the Catholics," she said. "I'm not like your father's family — so obsessed with being Presbyterians. Couldn't have lived across the street from the cathedral for eighty years and not had some fellow feeling for . . . But you can keep that under your hat when you're out at Nellie's." And then, "Poor old Dunny," she said. "For that matter, he probably needed all the blessing he could get."

Maybe she said that and maybe she didn't. I suppose it may just be that I have the memory now of wanting to sympathize with Dunny, consigned to the Catholic hell he hadn't thought of in decades, crushed under the slab set in place by the wife he hadn't seen for forty years.

"As for Julia's connection," my grandmother went on, "she was with him when he died. She buried him. If he'd wanted a priest, she'd have called one for him."

"Oh," I said. Now I began to remember. It was at The Forest that I had seen Miss Julia when I was a child, before Jamie and Aunt Marian lived there. She and "Cousin" Dunny, sitting on the long screened gallery when my other grandmother had taken us there to visit. Maybe that's where she was living when my father and his brothers lived at Longwood. But hadn't I seen her at Longwood, too?

"But why?" I said again. "What are you talking about?"

My grandmother's voice has almost left me now, imprinted though it was on my brain over and over again for almost half a lifetime. She couldn't carry a tune in a bucket, but there were lyric and dramatic qualities to her voice, a range in pitch when she was telling a story, an expressiveness . . . *Ah,* she seemed to be saying, *what I could tell you about this fascinating world! Ah, the perfidy of it! The high drama! The tragedy!* And *Oh, how ridiculous we all are, with our pretensions, how base with our betrayals. (Well, not us, usually, but sometimes even us.)*

There she sits, Grandmother One, in a green-painted, rush-bottomed rocking chair. It's afternoon and she's had her bath, carefully arranged her sparse white hair like a cap over her balding scalp and put on one of those thin, flower-sprigged voile dresses that old ladies used to wear in the spring and summer. Soon her daughters, my two aunts, will be home from work, bringing the day's gossip, but now she has plenty of time for me.

"Ah, Julia," she says. "What's the connection? Get me a cold biscuit, darling, and a glass of sherry, and I'll tell you. In the sideboard. Left-hand door."

She nibbled at her biscuit, sipped her afternoon sherry, gave me a sidelong glance. "Julia *lived* out there with Dunny," she said. "They lived for some years at Longwood, and then after she sold off the last of the farmland (or, I don't know, she may have lost it for taxes), and she still had a few cows, she rented part of The Forest—pastureland and house. She and Dunny and the cows moved there—Marian was living in town then."

"She and Dunny? . . ."

"They were cousins, of course," my grandmother said. "And I think he looked after the cows."

Saying "cows" seemed to imply something modest indeed, something far less lucrative than cattle. Well, I thought, that was the sort of thing people did in rural Adams County, Mississippi—never mind that he'd been on the grand tour with his bride, settled in Florence (in a palazzo?). When he came back to Natchez, he helped Julia look after her cows. What to make of all this? God knows, as my grandmother would say in moments of stress.

"But you must have seen him when Nellie would take you out to see Julia. Didn't she take you out there sometimes when you were children?"

"Yes," I said. "I remember going out there and I remember her coming to call."

*H*ere is Miss Julia coming to call on Grandmother Two. It's four o'clock on a summer afternoon in the late twenties.

Curious how one has very precise and vivid memories stamped on the gray cells—of people one has known only as friends of one's grown-up relatives, with whom one may never have had the least intimate personal connection. I remember, for example, one friend of my aunt's who wore extraordinary brilliant spots of orange rouge, round as dollars, on her cheeks, applied over a base of powder white as a geisha's face in a Gilbert and Sullivan opera. I remember her dumpy figure, her guttural voice, a mole on her chin, even her white tennis dress, as precisely as if she were my mother and I'd begun to memorize her on the day of my birth.

And I remember Miss Julia Nutt just as vividly.

Here she is, coming to call on my grandmother. People still called, still left calling cards in those days. Ladies, even poverty-stricken ladies (and gentlemen, too), continued to call.

I can't remember what she came in. Did she have a car? Did she drive it herself or did she have a chauffeur? In this strange world and time—the late twenties in the South—one might have a chauffeur whom one paid five dollars a week and keep. I have the impression that very poor white people might not be able to pay their taxes, but they could afford chauffeurs and cooks. Is that possible? But . . . I don't know—I recall that there were also very, very poor white people who had no chauffeurs, no cars, even, who drove themselves into town in their buggies to "call" or to shop. These people, however, were generally looked upon as curiosities. Perhaps they were just eccentric—opposed to peonage and the combustion engine.

I see them—Julia and Nellie—in the wide hall of my grandmother's house. They are embracing and then, together, arms about each other's waists, they're moving toward the horsehair-upholstered sofa in the parlor, then sitting side by side, bending toward each other, talking. In this memory I would have been seven or eight years old and they would both have been in their sixties— very old ladies in my view, and probably in their own, although my grandmother would live for another twenty-five years.

I hear the murmur of their voices. This grandmother's voice is softer, has a more limited range than the other's. She, too, is dressed in one of those flower-sprigged old-lady dresses—hers is always lavender and white, because she stays to the end of her life in semimourning for my grandfather, who at this point has been dead for five or six years. (Does anyone in the world besides me remember that lavender was the color for semimourning, put on after a year in black and two in black and white?)

I'm wandering. I want to tell about my memory of Miss Julia.

She's not in mourning. I'm sure she's not, although I don't recall her dress. I see instead the delicate band of ecru lace around her throat and the hint of lace at her wrists. She is erect, sturdy, high-bosomed, hawk-nosed, wattled—that's the detail that almost escaped me—her wattles half-concealed by the lace. Her softly wrinkled face is dusted, like the face of my aunt's tennis friend, with white powder. No round spots of rouge on her cheeks, though. Just the faintest hint of a flush. (I suppose I must have noticed these cosmetic details in part because they were unusual. Neither my grandmothers nor my mother wore rouge or lipstick, my grandmothers because it was not done by women of their generation, my mother because, she said, my father didn't like makeup.)

I hear Julia's voice. Husky. Does she smoke? I believe she does. Yes. I see her fit a cigarette into a holder and light it. But mainly I remember that delicate two-inch-wide band of ecru lace around her neck, and the lace, fragile as a cobweb, at her wrists.

Curious, I have no memory of eavesdropping on their conversation. I may, though, have begun to listen, lost interest, and fallen into a reverie of my own contriving. In my other grandmother's house conversations among grown people were dramatic. One listened. Drunken men staggered into her stories, flew into rages, tore up the very sheets on their beds or threw their shoes out the window. Game cocks were killed by mistake and put into the Sunday gumbo. The levee broke and the cotton fields flooded. Grooms left their brides abandoned at the altar. And there is this: Stories happened to people you knew. I was left with the distinct impression that the roomer who tore up his sheets was frustrated because my grandmother, a young widow at the time, refused to marry him.

But this grandmother, Grandmother Two, inquired of her friend whether the cows were calving or whether the lespedeza had been planted. Had the late freeze ruined the plums and figs this year? Would there be a pecan crop from that fifty-acre grove in the bend of the creek? They were both farmers, after all. Since my grandfather's death, Grandmother Two had supervised the operation of their farm. If these were the subjects of conversation, I would doubtless have lost interest.

I want to go back now to that afternoon's conversation with Grandmother One. I've gotten her a second glass of sherry and ferreted out the bourbon bottle and fixed myself a drink.

"They were third cousins," she said. "Or fifth. I'm not sure. You're distantly related to Dunny, too, of course. But no connection with the Nutts. She and Dunny must have been cousins on the other side. But *distant* cousins. If they'd been first cousins, almost like brother and sister, you know, there would never have been any talk. No one would dream that *first* cousins could . . . could . . ." She broke off.

"Do you mean they were lovers?"

"That's what everybody thought. But who am I to say? Judge not that ye be not judged. They had separate quarters, of course. Or so people said. At both places. He had his own rooms. This is hearsay, my dear. We were never intimate. I'm . . . Well, of course it isn't exactly hearsay. I'm telling you what Marian observed at The Forest. But, whatever the truth was, nobody called."

"What about you?" I said.

"We were never intimate," she said again. "But it was not an issue with me. You know. None of my business."

"But . . . *Nobody* called? You said Grandmother used to take us out there to see her. And she did. I remember."

"Oh, Nellie! I'm sure she never allowed a word spoken against Julia. Never."

And I was immediately sure of that, too. No word of censure was ever spoken against friend or kin in Nellie's house. No groom she knew would ever have left his bride at the altar. He'd sooner have had a heart attack and died. Not a year had passed since she had explained to me that a young cousin had not been to call for some months because he'd been on vacation in New Mexico. In fact, as Grandmother One had already told me, he and his lady friend had gotten drunk one evening in the cemetery — a lovely spot to share a drink, the loveliest cemetery in Mississippi — had stripped off their clothes to make love among the tombstones, and had been arrested for committing a public nuisance. He'd lost his job. She'd lost all her tennis students. Grandmother Two said he didn't come back from his vacation because he had found such a tempting opening out there he couldn't refuse it. I've forgotten what became of her.

Is there any point in digging up all these ancient scandals? Not only my grandmothers but those two insouciant lovers are long dead.

But they had to leave town. That's the point I'm making. They had to leave town because somebody caught them joyously fucking (and on his very own cemetery lot) in the middle of a beautiful, moonlit April night.

And Grandmother Two had to not know it happened.

Aside from that, what were the police doing harassing peaceful lovers in the middle of the night in the privacy of the cemetery?

Grandmother One was still thinking about Julia. "I'm not much of a caller," she said. "You know very well that I can't drive and never could afford a chauffeur. Here I sit on my front gallery in the six hundred block of Main Street, across from the cathedral, no distance from the Presbyterian church and the building and loan and Britton and Koontz Bank. Everybody eventually passes the house and they're always welcome to come in and visit." She sipped her sherry, raised her head as blind people often do, seeming to listen for some faint signal, or to sniff the air. "The young men used to go out to see Julia and Dunny in the evenings quite often," she said. "They were always fond of the young men."

What to make of that?

"Your father's bachelor party," she said. She said nothing else for a few minutes.

I waited.

"Your father's bachelor party was held at Longwood. Even I took a dim view of that." She was speaking of the drunken brawl held for the groom on the eve of his wedding. She shrugged and smiled as if to say, *I didn't really*. But instead she said, "I did."

The front gate creaked on its hinges. "Ah," she said, "Don't I hear the girls? Yes." The girls were my sixtyish aunts, coming home from their jobs as secretaries, one to the vice president of a bank, the other in an insurance agency.

I was left to consider the implications of my father's bachelor party.

There was no need for further questions. Grandmother One had made a clear statement. She had consigned Julia to the category of women who entertain men but not ladies. Shades of Belle Watling.

*B*ut I haven't done justice to the stories Grandmother Two used to tell—or rather read aloud to us children. True, they were not about real people—there was never the baffling but fascinating glimpse into the crisis-plagued world of our own grown-up family. But all the same, they rivaled in thrills the tale of the roomer who tore up his sheets and threw his shoes out the window.

Grandmother Two's characters were distant and mythical people and her stories had shape—endings and, at least implicitly, morals. There was the Covenanter ancestor whose sister—when he fled her house pursued by King Charles's troops—concealed under her layered and voluminous skirts the League and the Covenant signed in the blood of the dissenters. There were the two children who wandered away from their lonely forest homestead and were murdered by Indians. And there was the gypsy boy picked up by a tornado from his family's caravan and dropped in the lap of a wilderness bandit from whom he was rescued by a pious countrywoman who promptly began to teach him his Catechism. In one of these tales a stern father, crippled by gout, can't pursue his daughter and her forbidden lover when they flee like Lochinvar and his bride into the wild Mississippi night, moss blowing, limbs creaking, owls screaming in the darkness. But the storm pur-

sues them—wind is precursor to downpour. Crossing
the Homochitto River, the lovers are swept away in one
of those flash floods that rush without warning out of
the Southern hills.

Sometimes in Grandmother Two's stories the heroes
and heroines are animals: a boy frog named Joe who repeatedly gets into trouble from which he is rescued by
Mrs. Crow, a splendid elderly crow lady in a bonnet and
black shawl; a trickster rabbit escaped from the circus,
shivering under the Chickasaw rose hedge; a bear who
has gnawed off his toe to escape a trap.

Vengeful Catholics. Stern fathers. Disobedient daughters. Murderous Indians. Animals escaping the devices
men have made to entrap and kill them. These were
Grandmother Two's characters, and she thought about
them, wrote down their stories, and read them to us
after dinner on weekday afternoons, or on weekday
evenings at bedtime.

Sundays, after Sunday School and church and Sunday dinner (Grandmother carving the leg of lamb; dig-
nified, officious Hampton, Grandmother's chauffeur,
now in his white waiter's jacket, handing the biscuits
and rice and butter beans, tapioca pudding for dessert),
story reading was strictly from the Bible or the *Christian
Observer*. Dominoes and checkers, croquet sets and packs
of cards, had vanished on Saturday night into closets and

drawers. The Sunday funnies were put away to be read on Monday. If we were staying with Grandmother Two, our mother usually fled with us after dinner to Grandmother One, where you could read the funnies, play a game of Parcheesi, and go to the Prentiss Club for an afternoon swim.

Those old Covenanters might seem to me to be as made-up as Bluebeard, but I was aware that their heavy hands still pressed down on my grandmother's shoulders.

Since I began a month or so ago thinking about Julia and Dunbar and Nellie, I have gone back to Natchez. I've gone to the cemeteries at The Forest and at Longwood. Julia, I've discovered, is indeed buried in the Longwood cemetery, just a short walk into the woods from that astonishing five-storied octagonal mansion with its copper-colored dome and carved finial. She's surrounded by her kin—parents and cousins and the two nephews who inherited the house and sold it to buy food and clothes and whisky.

She is visited now by thousands of callers, tourists who come from all over the world to see the house—widely advertised as a gem of Sloan architecture—and who wander in the woods and visit the cemetery and pay their respects to the dead.

I've looked at old photographs and gotten out boxes of letters still in the possession of me and my siblings. Photographs: In the one of Grandmother Two that I like best she stands in the photographer's studio, trim and narrow waisted in a formal riding habit and top hat, a tasseled crop in her gloved hands. The skirt of her habit (of course she rode sidesaddle) falls in graceful folds. The trim jacket is buttoned up to the barely visible starched collar of her blouse with eighteen fabric-covered buttons and fastened at the throat with what appears to be a silver brooch in the shape of a riding whip. Tendrils of dark curly hair escape under the stiff brim of her hat. She is poised, self-possessed, gentle, a half-smile on her lovely, strong, intelligent young face. She can't be more than seventeen or eighteen. In another, she's a married woman seated at a spinet surrounded by her four sons, who gaze with uniform wide-eyed solemnity sideways toward the photographer. Nellie, her sad face in profile, her hair piled high and twisted into a French knot, looks at her sons. She wears a high-necked blouse in the style of the time, with long, cuffed, leg-o'-mutton sleeves. I can barely make out, propped on the lid of the spinet, a dim picture—it seems to be of a reclining child surrounded by flowers. On either end of the lid are small bronze figures—one of a mounted Roman general, the other of a woman carrying a water pitcher on her shoulder. I deduce from the apparent ages of the boys that this photograph of Nellie and her children must have been made not long after the death of her only daughter, Corinne, at the age of five.

I've seen a photograph of Julia, too, as a young woman, standing next to Nellie in a large group of tennis players who are disposed about a lawn, some standing, some sitting, in front of a columned house. She holds a tennis racquet in one hand and looks directly into the camera. But her face is blurred. I can't make out either the features or the expression.

I have read the letters exchanged between Nellie and John Ayres, her husband-to-be, during their courtship and engagement, and later, after their marriage, when for periods of weeks or months he was away working in a commission merchant's office in New Orleans and she was at home, either in town with her parents (this during the latter months of a pregnancy) or in the deep country on their farm.

Almost every one of the playful early letters refers to Julia: "My best friend," or "Julia sends her love and a saucy message which I won't relay," or "Julia's lieutenant is here." (Or "is gone," or "came to call.") Often in these letters she uses Julia or her sister, Corinne, as a surrogate for herself: "Corinne tells me to say that she longs to see you—hopes you'll soon return to our little town." Or "Julia sends you . . ." not just a saucy message, but sometimes even a kiss. "Julia," she writes, "isn't the kind of girl to be deeply distressed about any man, I reckon." Of herself in one of the early letters she writes, "I am a very cold woman and would not have you deceive yourself by thinking otherwise." "My dear Mr. Ayres," she addresses him in the courtship letters, and signs herself, "Your friend, Nellie Henderson." Later she writes, "My dear Jack," but still signs herself, "Your friend."

Almost from the beginning he is direct, passionate. "My darling Nellie," he writes. "My own dear Nellie." And "You cannot imagine how much I love you," and "I would not have you believe me perfect nor rich . . . You would be all I would have to live and work for." And (perhaps after the "cold woman" letter) "I love you too much to have you marry one you do not love and there is no sacrifice I would not make to save you from such an act."

The formal games of courtship continue into the engagement. She pretends, for example, not to know why he asks for her hand size. (Gloves, in those days, like candy and flowers, were acceptable gifts from a man to a young lady.)

Suddenly, after more than three years (There is a period in the middle from which no letters remain. If he was in Natchez, maybe none were written), they are engaged and then married. "My dear Jack" becomes "My darling husband," "My dearest Jack" (this in a period when women customarily called their husbands Mister), and, to me even more moving, "My dear old man." One deduces that the cold woman has melted.

Julia is still a presence in these later letters. Nellie takes the babies and goes to Longwood to spend the day. But the correspondence centers now on planting time and harvest, on the chickens, the turkeys, the cows (Lillie Langtry, their soft-eyed Jersey, has calved), on the scarcity of money, on the children: "Richardson is asleep and Sister is rocking the baby," and, overwhelmingly, on her loneliness when he is away: "I long for the day when you'll never have to leave me again." About Julia's romances, her "beaus," Nellie falls silent. What happened to the lieutenant? Did she spurn him? Did he abandon her? Or was he, in fact, Dunbar Marshall? I don't know. But what happened eventually, as we know from Dunbar's tombstone, as well as from ancient gossip, is that he married Fanny Bullitt.

What I didn't know—what neither Miss Adah nor Grandmother One told me and what I found out when I began looking at old records and writing about these lives—is that not only were Julia and Dunbar "distant cousins," but Julia and Fanny were first cousins.

Now I am trying to fit this fact into my ancient romance.

Did Fanny steal Julia's lover away? Is that the tragedy unrecorded in Nellie's letters?

As I gather the fragments of this story, I have a choice: I could invent—I am a novelist, after all, accustomed to inventing. I imagine that Fanny was yielding and soft and treacherous, that she feigned innocence and stupidity and helplessness. I could set her off against Julia, whom I remember so well as a sturdy, deep-voiced old woman, and think of as the young woman of whom Nellie had said, "Julia isn't the kind of girl to be deeply distressed about any man, I reckon." The temptation is seductive. I would like to be able to tell you of Fanny's betrayal of her cousin, of Dunbar's escape from a hateful marriage, of her refusal to divorce him, of the climax: Julia's defiance of convention when she welcomes him to her house, her arms, her bed. And, finally, of how Fanny, after Dunny is dead, comes back to claim him, to put her name on his gravestone in a last furious act of possession—how God and the Catholic Church are mere excuses for the acting out of rage and jealousy and a rivalry begun perhaps when the two women were children. Julia was cleverer, more lovable, stronger, nobler, and Fanny! . . . You see? I almost can't resist it.

But this is fiction—romantic nonsense. All I know

is that Dunny left his wife, came back to Adams County, moved somehow into Julia's life, began "looking after her cows" and occupying his own quarters in her house. I have heard that no one called except Nellie and the young men. And I know that, in defiance of her church and his marriage vows, they committed themselves to each other and for a lifetime honored their commitment.

Yes, *her* church. Like Fanny, Julia was born a Catholic.

Later there are wills from which one can perhaps make reasonable deductions. There was Longwood — and the eventual disposal of Longwood must have been on a number of minds. It belonged to Julia and its value as a curiosity, as a family property, as a tourist attraction (toward the end of her life when Natchez houses were beginning to be famous) would have been evident to the nieces and nephews who did in fact inherit it at her death and who later sold it. One of the nephews, I recall, was living there as a kind of caretaker and guide during the years of my adolescence. One deduces, therefore, that Julia did not fall out with her family to the extent of disinheriting them. Perhaps, after all, they — the nephews in any case — were among "the young men" who continued to call.

Dunny left a will, too, as I discovered, nosing around

the chancery clerk's office. His estate was modest, but not so modest as I had expected it to be, thinking of him as the man who looked after Julia's cows—and her other needs. Some twenty thousand dollars in securities went to his daughter. Daughter? Where did she come from? No one had mentioned her. Fanny and the daughter will remain shadows to the end of this story.

As I've observed, Dunbar is not mentioned in Julia's will. But, surprisingly (to me), my great-aunt Marian and her husband, Jamie, are mentioned. The will states that Marian and Jamie are honorable and trustworthy people and they are appointed appraisers of the real property.

Nor is Julia mentioned in Dunbar's will.

It is impossible for me to resist the supposition that the two of them talked to each other of their wills, that perhaps they decided together to let community and family finally have their due.

Here is another vivid memory from my early childhood. It's summer and as usual we are visiting Grandmother Two. I see myself sitting beside her in the back seat of her old dark green Buick. At this point, if I am a small child, the Buick is, in fact, not very old. Grandmother Two didn't lose her husband's money until the failure of the Hibernia Bank in the early years of the Great Depression. Thereafter, her car got older and older. Hampton's chauffeur's uniform and the car's paint faded together to an acid purplish green; but he managed to keep the car alive for years. In any case, Hampton is driving us to town. Now, he has parked in front of the columned temple of Britton and Koontz Bank. He has opened the door and bowed Grandmother out. She is wearing her white-and-lavender, flower-sprigged summer dress and white cotton gloves and carrying a little white crocheted drawstring pouch—her reticule. Then we are at home again. She must have cashed a check to pay Hampton, or Ida, the cook, or the vegetable man—or all three. For some reason money is about to change hands in the house and she must count it out and handle it.

We are in the bathroom now and I am standing by the basin watching a process that takes place every time money comes into the house.

"Why?" I am asking.

She has removed her gloves. Her arms are bare to the elbows. She is bent seriously over the basin, but she turns toward me to answer my question, to tell me about germs and filth.

She is washing the money.

A few dimes and quarters and fifty-cent pieces lie glinting at the bottom of the basin. A number of bills

(Ones and fives probably. I'm sure I would have noticed tens. Tens were scarcer in those days than hundreds would be now) float limply above the coins, and Grandmother picks them up and soaps them and rubs them together. She stirs the water in the basin and the coins clink against each other. She drains the basin. She rinses the coins and bills and lays them out on a towel to dry.

Grandmother Two is not crazy. She is a sane and gentle lady who manages a farm (her husband and sister-in-law are dead now) and a complex household consisting of her sister, her servants, and, this summer day, three grandchildren and a pregnant daughter-in-law. (I'm choosing for this memory the summer of my brother's birth.) Dinner is served every day at one. Hampton puts on his white waiter's jacket and hands the corn bread, removes the plates, brings in the dessert (tapioca pudding again). After dinner we may play a game of casino, or she may read us one of her stories. Or we may wind the music box that sits on the old square piano and listen to "Humoresque." Or pretend that the scatter rugs in the long, cool hall are pirate ships and mount an invasion of the parlor. At four Hampton will close the downstairs shutters and depart. Suppertime will come and Grandmother and Mother will make tomato sandwiches and cut us each a piece of Ida's delicious sponge cake for dessert.

But, nevertheless, it's true that she washes every coin and bill that passes through her hands.

Can money be washed clean? Can we drive the money changers from the temple?

Has this anything to do with Julia? With the cousin who went permanently vacationing in New Mexico?

*H*ere is one of Grandmother Two's stories. This one she did not write down. But she told it to us—and not only she but my great-aunt Corinne, her sister, also told it to us. And since it was told in turn to my older sister, my younger sister, my brother, and me, as we each got old enough to hear and understand it, I heard it many times. It seems to me now that it is the link between her written-down stories and a world in which every coin must be washed before it can be touched.

In the early nineteenth century Samuel Brooks and his wife, Mary, had two daughters (or family tradition says they did. I haven't checked the cemetery for their stones). Mr. Brooks was the first American mayor of Natchez, and another legend has it that in his Presbyterian zeal he closed down all the taverns and whorehouses and "gambling dens" of Natchez-under-the-Hill (as notorious along the river in its time as the stews of London) and that the gamblers and pimps and prostitutes and riverboat men marched on his house to rout him out and force him to rescind his order, or else to kill him. One family myth (so bizarre that it may possibly be true) is that a rock crashed through an upstairs window and that when Mrs. Brooks went to the window and saw and heard the mob, she began to scream. She screamed and screamed (rocks flying, presumably, windows shattering), until she burst a blood vessel in her throat and bled to death. Family tradition does not record whether Mr. Brooks rescinded his order.

Never mind about that. The story I want to tell is about the daughters who, to make a long story short, were to attend their first ball as young ladies, escorted, as was customary in those days, by their parents.

I think of Tolstoy's joyous young heroines, doomed also to undergo great trials, of Katya and Natasha at their first balls; and I think of my own first evening wrap—a scarlet woolen cape with gold braid frogs on the shoulders, a dramatic cape that swept the floor when I made my entrance at a dance.

So: Ball gowns had been ordered—from Worth, from Paris! Or so I seem to recall; but I must have made that up. The silks and braid, the velvets and peau de soie and moiré taffeta, probably came up on a riverboat from New Orleans, and the seamstress perhaps was "French"

—a mulatto slave woman. Or, who knows, Mrs. Brooks herself may have been skilled at needlework, as my own Grandmother One was.

The young ladies came down the stairs. I pictured them, as the tale was told, sweeping down the broad staircase in my grandmother's house in town, stairs that descended into a high-ceilinged parlor and airy open hallway. But they lived, in fact, in an earlier, Spanish-period house with low ceilings and narrow, enclosed stairs like a ship's companion.

Father and Mother awaited them in the drawing room, admired their gowns, had them turn round to be inspected on all sides. Mother adjusted the lace of a shawl, tucked in an errant curl. Did she know what was about to happen? Surely not.

And then the old man—the father, the Presbyterian elder, the sadist—folded his arms and addressed them. Was his voice gentle? His mien fatherly? "And now, young ladies," he said. "Go upstairs. Take off your ball gowns and go to bed. You must learn to bear disappointment."

One of those young ladies was Grandmother Two's grandmother. Who else could have passed along this story, made this comment on the character of Mr. Brooks—her father?

*H*ere, I think about the lives of women in that long, long ago time when marriage was the only career open to ladies. I think of all those real and fictional tyrannical nineteenth-century fathers and I begin to think of my grandmother's maiden sister and maiden sister-in-law, who, for their own reasons, used their own strategems to avoid marriage—and stratagems they did have, or Corinne did, I know, because my father has told me about them.

These women led busy, active, devout lives. One had her own money (half of the inheritance that enabled Grandfather to buy the house in town) and she helped him run the struggling farm, which belonged to them jointly. Often she stayed there alone, far out in the country, a mile from the nearest white family, when Grandfather was away and Grandmother Two was pregnant and staying in town with her parents. The other, Corinne, taught for a while (speech and elocution to young ladies, and of course Sunday School). She gardened and called and read. (By the time I came along, her favorite author was Edgar Rice Burroughs, her hero John Carter, Warlord of Mars.) She looked after her aging parents and helped her sister raise four boys, all of whom regarded her, I know, as a second mother.

I think about them—these women—and I think about my grandmother and the lovely letters addressed to "Dearest Jack," to "My darling husband," "My dear old man."

And I think about the courage and passion of Julia Nutt.

What's essential, too, is to remember and understand, if we can, the depth and conviction and rootedness of Grandmother Two's piety and the virulence of ancestral hatred of the Catholic Church.

I see again, on the sewing table by her brown wicker rocker, her worn Bible, the gilt mostly gone from the page edges and from the letters stamped on its limp leather cover; and I remember how each morning she closed her bedroom door to read and pray. We were not allowed to disturb her then.

I recall the reading aloud of Bible stories on Sunday evening—stories of how Elisha called out the bears to eat the children who made fun of him; of how Jehovah drowned the armies of Pharaoh; of how, over and over again, the Israelites did evil in the sight of the Lord and were delivered into the hands of the Ammonites or the Moabites or the Philistines. And later, how, when God relented, the Israelites fell on them (whoever they were) and slew them every one.

But Ruth, too, and Naomi. Ruth, who said, "Intreat me not to leave thee."

I recall again the mention in the Henderson Bible of those long-dead dissenters who "suffered much in the persecution of the church . . ."

And I remember my own visit years ago to Scotland, remember seeing the wreckage, the devastation of ancient abbeys and churches, the statues of saints left noseless and sometimes headless and armless by the furious dissenters. I had gone earlier to Italy, had seen San Clemente and San Pietro in Vincoli and Santa Costanza and the duomos in Florence and Siena—the glittering mosaics, the carved pulpits, the great silver candelabra—and also the small, homely, pious men and women going about their tasks—sowing seed, plowing, baking, building—on the panels around the Campanile in Florence.

And then, later, in Scotland, to see the awful noseless faces, the ruined abbey walls . . . Ah, they were jagged stones in the middle of my life, even far as I believed myself to be from all those ancient passions.

Nellie had been born a Henderson, a collateral descendant of Alexander Henderson, the Scottish divine who debated and prayed with Charles I for days, seeking his renunciation of the Catholic faith, and who, when he failed, turned the king over to Cromwell, "to be murdered," as Miss Adah said. Henderson, some church historians record, took to his bed afterwards and never got up. Seven days later he died of grief. Others give a different account of his death.

For Nellie, the Covenanter has signed the League and the Covenant in his blood. His sister has concealed it on her person. The runaway lovers must drown. The straying children must be murdered. The young ladies must learn to bear disappointment.

I come now to Julia's death and burial and the mystery that surrounds them.

She lived only two years after Dunny: Both died relatively young—in their early sixties. I think she must have moved back to Longwood when he died. That may be why I remember climbing among the joists and rafters there. Perhaps she sold her cattle and gave up farming, since she no longer had him to help her with the cows. In any case, the snapshot of my sister and me on Jamie's donkey tells me that by the time I was ten or so, Jamie and Marian lived at The Forest. I was ten in 1931, the year after Dunny's death, the year before Julia's.

But it's the funerals that puzzle me—the role the Catholic and Presbyterian Churches played, or didn't play, in both these deaths—the funerals, and Nellie's part in them.

Remember that Julia and Dunny—one born into the Catholic Church, the other a convert "for convenience" during his brief marriage—lived all their adult lives in what their church regarded as mortal sin.

Who decided to bury Dunny at The Forest? Surely it was Julia, not Marian. Who conducted the service? Not a priest, according to Miss Adah. Marian said that he had had a Presbyterian funeral and if that was not good enough to get him into heaven, he could just go the other way. Did she say this out of loyalty to Julia and Dunny, out of knowledge of their private convictions? Or possibly—this has just occurred to me—she knew the history of his marriage and took a genuine pleasure in foiling his wife, whom she believed to be the villain of the piece.

And then: *Presbyterian?* Where would Julia have found, in that rigid world, a Presbyterian minister willing to say his church's service over her fallen-away Catholic lover?

There are no answers to these questions but they are enough to set the novelist off in half a dozen different directions.

Perhaps—can it be—there was only Julia following his coffin to the dark, crumbling cemetery, only Julia standing by as the grave was filled.

Or perhaps Nellie was with her. It may be that Nellie brought her worn Bible and read a psalm and said a prayer.

It has struck me more than once, thinking about these lives, that Julia, out of deep knowledge of her friend's character, may, to shield her from distress, have concealed from Nellie the depth of hers and Dunny's indifference to what anybody's church said or believed or attempted to enforce in the community they lived at the edge of. She was never "the kind of girl to be deeply distressed about any man." Or about any church? Or community ostracism? Not those either, perhaps. But about her friend's concern for their souls? That may have been another matter.

Again I must resist making up their story.

Two years passed. Julia died. Her funeral was held in my grandmother's parlor. It was conducted by a priest. But of course (outside the church, in a Protestant house) no mass could be said.

How do I know this? I know it only because my mother chanced to tell me—years after my conversation with Grandmother One about the scandal of Julia and Dunny's life together. Such a funeral was strange enough for her to remark on it, to speculate about why, to suggest that Julia, because of her life, was denied burial from the cathedral. (We lived at the time in a small town in a neighboring state and, from what my mother said, neither she nor my father were privy to the funeral arrangements or went to the funeral.)

"That must have been the only time a priest ever entered your grandmother's house," she said.

A priest. Why did Nellie call in a priest? Is it believable even for a moment that after Dunny's death Julia went back into the Catholic Church, believable that she could call her whole life a sin and do penance for it? That would be one explanation, wouldn't it, for the priest? But such a thing is not believable, and for more than speculative reasons. If she had gone to confession, if she had been absolved, the lost lamb returned to the fold, she would have been buried from the cathedral with a proper mass.

"I've heard of cases like that in those days," a priest friend of mine said, when I asked him to speculate about what might have happened. "If the dead woman was known to be an unrepentant sinner and church burial was out of the question, some kind father might be willing to sneak in the back door and say a prayer over the body—wherever it was. No. It isn't surprising."

"What's surprising is who called him in," I said.

Why did Nellie call in a priest? Did honor somehow require it? Or could she find no one else, no one in her own or any other church to stand beside her and say a prayer at her friend's coffin?

• • •

I am sure now that I remember my grandmother and Julia—and Dunny, too—on the gallery at The Forest on a long, hot summer afternoon. I recall an embrace and then the two women in intimate, quiet conversation. I hear their soft voices, Julia's pitched a shade lower than my grandmother's, the voices, it seems to me now, of ghosts, alive only in my head and only for the time left to me to remember them. I remember the call and response of those voices as I might remember music—the oboe making room for the flute and then meditatively answering—and, like oboe and flute, they speak with deep emotion, but wordlessly.

Dunny sits a little apart from the women, dressed in shabby khaki pants and a collarless shirt. Is he perhaps smoking a pipe, having first asked the ladies' permission? Hampton, I think, sits in the kitchen. I hear his deep officious voice, condescending as a tuba. He, too, is in quiet conversation, with whoever presides over Julia's household.

The evening draws in. My sister and I come back from exploring the graveyard and the ruined foundation of the old house. I hear the locusts' stridulant passionate calls rise and fall from tree to tree, as I have heard them all my life from the tree-shadowed galleries of the South.

Does it matter at all whether I recall or imagine this scene?

There they are. I *know* they are there, the three of them together, making their mysterious music. I want to convey the quality of their lives, of their friendship, but I cannot. The secrets of a lifetime stand between me and them.

Instead I keep returning in my mind to one of the last times I spoke with Grandmother Two. She was ninety-one. Afterwards I saw her only when she was very ill, dying. She walked with me—tottered—toward the front door to see me out. Jintzy, the black sitter who looked after her those last feeble years, alert to prevent a fall, hovered in the background. Grandmother steadied herself on my arm.

I bent and kissed her crumpled tissue paper cheek, told her I'd come again soon.

"You're married, aren't you?" she said anxiously. And then, "Of course. You were married *here*. I remember now."

"Yes," I said.

"All those camellias," she said. "I remember all those beautiful camellias."

"Yes. January. They were in full bloom."

She gripped my arm with a strong old claw. "Have lots of children, darling," she said. "Have lots of children."

We were indeed married in her house. I came down the stairs in an ivory satin gown and sweeping veil of peau de soie, as I had so often imagined those two unfortunate young ladies coming down for their first ball.

Lots of children? Grandmother was confused, of course. I already had three sons.

But . . . Perhaps she was going back to the joyous and difficult and tragic years when her own boys were growing up, when her daughter died. Perhaps she was still wondering and grieving for her sister's single life. Or perhaps she was thinking of Julia, who never had a child, could never have had a child.

When I saw her last, propped on a high hospital bed, dying of pneumonia, "the old man's friend," as people used to say, she was barely conscious, murmuring, whispering something I could not make out.

Jintzy sat nodding, half-asleep, in a chair against the wall. My great-aunt Corinne sat in the brown wicker rocker with a Bible in her lap. She was reading aloud. All the time I stood by the bed she continued to read, or, sometimes, lifting her ancient, ravaged, tear-streaked face, to repeat from memory: "Hear my prayer, O Lord, and let my cry come unto thee. Hide not thy face from me . . ."

"Juh . . . juh . . . juh . . ." my grandmother was whispering. "Juh . . . juh . . . juh . . ." Hardly more than a breath.

". . . and my days are like a shadow that declineth; and I am withered like grass . . ."

Over and over again: "Juh . . . juh . . . juh . . ."

"So the heathen shall fear the name of the Lord . . ."

Jack? Her darling Jack? Her dear old man? Or Julia?

But no, it was Jintzy for whom she called, when she finally spoke. "Jintzy," she said. "Jintzy, Jintzy, Jintzy, Jintzy."

For the rest she was silent still.

*H*AMPTON

All . . . demolish . . . burn . . .
I gain control . . . I suffer . . .
shameful . . . O! [a person's name] . . .

> —Alkaios
> fragment from Papyri Oxyrhyncus

I

I STILL SEE HAMPTON ELLIOT, wearing his gardener's khakis and boots, standing in the little oval garden behind my grandmother's house, leaning on a hoe, his head tilted to the side. He is listening patiently to my great-aunt, a maiden lady in her sixties. I am a child, watching them from above, looking out the dining room window down the slope toward the garden. There is something of importance to be settled: what to do about the blight on the gardenias; when the night-blooming cereus may bloom. Hampton is listening, but surely he already knows exactly what he will do and how to do it. Then, all of a sudden, he raises his hoe and brings it down fiercely into the grass behind and to the left of my aunt. He chops again and I lean out and see something thrashing in the grass. He has killed a snake.

My aunt shrinks back. Then she flips open her pince-nez, holds it to her eyes, and looks down happily at the writhing snake. "Kill him," she says. "Oh, he's not dead yet, Hampton. Kill him."

Over the course of the next week or two the snake grows longer and more venomous, the tale more dramatic. "I hate to think, if Hampton hadn't been there, been so alert," my aunt says. "I might have been bitten. Yes. I think it was a copperhead. Wasn't it? And right behind me. I might have been *killed!*"

Now I see Hampton standing by my grandmother's car, a seven-passenger dark green Buick parked outside the Presbyterian church in Natchez on a Sunday morning. He wears his black chauffeur's jacket and visored cap and he's lifting the cap from his head, wiping away sweat with a white handkerchief. We are emerging from the cool twilight of the church into the glare of a hot July noon. Heat and light shimmer up from the street. Hampton ushers my grandmother and great-aunt Corinne and my older sister into the car, flips up the jump seats for my younger sister and me, and opens the front door for my brother. "Here's the little man," he says. "In you go."

"Home, Hampton," my grandmother says.

He gets into the car and I see the back of his neck, dark brown and creased and shaven, his cap, settled firmly on his head, and his hands, large and competent, on the wheel. I don't remember that he speaks again.

Hampton worked for my grandmother and her sister, Corinne, as director of the household, butler, chauffeur, mechanic, gardener, and handyman during the years of my childhood, and continued to work for them until they died, a year or so apart at the ages of ninety and ninety-one. That is, from 1931 until 1953 or 1954.

He was not one to cater to children. He had no interest in amusing us when we visited my grandmother —my recollection of him is that his attitude toward us was sometimes preoccupied, sometimes condescending, and that it was tinged with a touch of falsity. I think particularly of his laugh. It was his laugh—a cross between a chuckle and a kind of staccato nasal bray—that seemed false to me. But maybe I was wrong. It may be that he was a man who had no interest in other people's children, or that children were not a part of his job. In any case he went about his business without paying more than minimal attention to us four—my two sisters, my brother, and me.

As I grow older, the past is an increasing weight in the balance scale of my life, and the present lighter, ephemeral. The dust of the present blows away, the past grows more real, heavier: Hampton's brown skin and shaven head, my great-aunt's pince-nez, her story of the flood in the rice fields, my uncle's auburn hair and high color. But although I call up these memories, although they are my own, I have reservations. I know that I put words in the mouths of people who did not speak them. I imagine scenes at which I was not present. I know that this is my world and no one else's —my stories, my history. Or myth, perhaps, one among the myths that form the lives of families and sometimes of larger worlds.

I should say, too, that everyone who cared about these events is dead. I do not believe that any living person can be hurt either by the truth or by the fiction in my stories. Hampton is dead, my aunt, my grandmother, my uncles. I'm an old woman.

Now I recall a scene from the 1940s. I am a young married woman. I see Hampton serving dinner, wearing his white waiter's jacket. Yes, we are all grown people, and my sister and brother-in-law and I are visiting my grandmother with a friend, a young doctor from South Alabama who had gone to medical school with my brother-in-law. Gold-framed portraits of ladies and gentlemen (our great- and great-great-grandparents), executed with varying degrees of skill by itinerant nineteenth-century painters, look down at us from the dining room walls. The Aaron Willard clock on the mantel chimes one o'clock. A steaming leg of lamb, already carved and handed around, sits in front of my grandmother. Hampton's shaven scalp gleams under the light from the chandelier and his expression is intent. He is offering a silver sauceboat to our guest. The time is just after the end of the Second World War and broccoli has only recently penetrated the Deep South market and begun to appear on tables where one used to see butter beans and turnip greens and cabbage and other home-grown vegetables, but few exotica. "Butter for your broccoli, Dr. McCloud," Hampton says in a low, breathy, conspiratorial voice. He has decided that Dr. McCloud is too provincial ever to have seen broccoli before. Maybe he's never even seen a sauceboat.

"Lord, Lord," Bull McCloud said to us afterwards. "He saw the hayseeds in my hair, knew I was nothing but a South Alabama country boy."

During those years my relationship with Hampton changed. I didn't see him often — just for conversations during brief visits to my grandmother and, in the years after her death and, a year later, my great-aunt's death, two or three calls at the local nursing home where he spent his last years. But at that time he had decided that he wanted to tell me about his life — his life as a boy growing up, as a man before he came to my grandmother, and as a fixture in my grandmother's household. He wanted to tell me, not about his personal life, but about his life among white people. He always chose, as it seemed to me, illustrations that made a point. There was nothing trivial in his stories.

For one thing, he knew that I was a writer. Perhaps he was deliberately giving me material. For another, by the time he was in the nursing home, the years of the Civil Rights battles were well under way. Legislation had been passed and the regulations governing federal grants meant that the nursing home was integrated, a forced departure from Southern mores and taboos that would have been unthinkable ten years earlier. So perhaps what he felt—as if the crumbling loess of our land had shifted and compacted and risen under his feet— was the shift of power toward him and his people. His vote would count, so to speak, and he meant to cast it in his home precinct. And finally, he was old. Age may in his own mind have freed him from the necessity for caution, particularly caution in his behavior with young white women.

He grew up, he told me, in Tensas Parish, Louisiana. His mother was house servant to an elderly bachelor who owned considerable land in the parish, as well as a cotton gin that served him and the surrounding farmers. I think, from the stories Hampton passed along to me about this gentleman, that he must have been indifferent to the opinions of his peers, aloof from the local society—what my mother might have called a law unto himself.

Hampton's mother had taught him to read and write and calculate when he was a very young child. "My mother could read and write," he told me, "but except for that, as to the way we lived, we were no different from other country colored people at that time. Our house was papered with newspaper for insulation. Walls were my primers." He never mentioned his father and he always spoke matter-of-factly—no side-glances to see how I might take what he said. "I was working full-time by the time I was twelve," he said. "First in the kitchen, then serving. I could read, though, and add and subtract, so he—our employer—came to depend on me somewhat more than he might have otherwise.

"Well," Hampton said, "he was a sport. Owned the first automobile in the parish—ordered it and some drums of gasoline and a supply of oil from a catalogue. It came in on the train to the nearest station, across the river in Natchez. He sent for me and we went in to get it—me in the wagon and him on horseback—loaded it onto the wagon and took it to the country. You should have seen us rolling onto the ferry—car shiny and black, sitting up high in the bed of the wagon, mules pulling us, me in the driver's seat, him on his horse ahead of us. The people must have thought he was crazy.

"Well, we unloaded the car in the pasture," Hampton said. The old man had some directions that came with it. "What was it? A Model T? No, it was before Model T's. I put the gasoline in, and the oil and water, and cranked it up and we got in and taught ourselves to drive it, and then we taught ourselves to take care of it." He laughed his nasal, staccato, nervous, condescending laugh. "Driving around the parish, he would scare horses into the ditch," he said. "Took pleasure in that. He was—yes, I guess he was what you might call a sport.

"He must have got that car when I was about fifteen, because it was the next year he sent me off to school. 'You need to learn more about figuring,' is what he told me, and he sent me over the river up north of Natchez to Alcorn College. The end of that school year, June, I came home, went to his house to pay my respects. He didn't live like your grandmother—I mean he wasn't formal, serving dinner in the dining room, calling on the neighbors. His office was his living room and often as not he pushed the papers off the daybed and slept on it. This day he's sitting there at his desk, desk piled with papers and books, looks like he's been trying to get things straight. 'Well, Hamp,' he says to me, 'what did they teach you over there?' 'I learned single-entry bookkeeping, sir,' I say. He looks down at that mess of papers and laughs. 'You better go back next year and learn double-entry,' he says. So I did."

After that Hampton went to work in the gin. By the time he was twenty-two or twenty-three he was running the gin. By the time he was thirty he was running the farm. I suppose he would have been called the straw boss or hostler or some such title, not manager or even foreman—those would be white men's titles. But in truth he was the CEO.

"Away from home, the old man liked to cut a figure," he said to me. "He'd go down to New Orleans, up to Memphis, to the races. He liked to gamble. He was gone a considerable part of the year—left me in charge. But I will say he always kept a close eye on operations. He saw that the animals were looked after. He studied the figures. He read the farm journals and bought the best equipment. For the rest of it—parceling out the crops, deciding when to plant and when to lay by, settling up, keeping the books—I saw to that."

This was during the years when farms in the South were run on the sharecropping system. A tenant family, usually black, farmed thirty or forty acres, the owner furnished seed and fertilizer and credit at the commissary, and profits, if any, were shared after the harvest. The old man's farm—or plantation, as anything over a hundred acres used to be called in those parts—was around two thousand acres of prime Delta land, Hampton said. So there were probably fifty to sixty families on it, depending on how much of the land was cultivable.

In 1931 the old man died quite suddenly of a heart attack or stroke. The beneficiaries of his will were a couple of nephews who lived in the North and who came down and cleared out and sold everything in the house, sold the house, the land, and the gin. Hampton had never seen them before. He was not mentioned in the will.

It was 1931. To say that to someone of my generation is like tolling the church bell for a funeral.

He was forty-five years old. He was married and by then he must have had a child. His mother was probably dead. Later, all the time I knew him (until, in his old age, he was crippled by arthritis and got hugely fat), he seemed not to grow older. He was always vigorous, a little overweight, his scalp shaven, his smooth brown face shining. He carried his stomach high and he'd be dressed in his uniform, his disguise—whatever his current role required: waiter's jacket, chauffeur's cap and dark blazer, or gardener's khakis and boots. Perhaps the uniforms masked the changes brought about by age. One didn't look past them.

He never talked of his wife and daughter to me and I never saw either of them.

Now here's something I hadn't thought of before. During the Depression, a year or two after Hampton came to work for her, after she lost every penny she had in the failure of the Hibernia Bank in New Orleans, my grandmother and her maiden sister, Corinne (who never had money of her own other than what she had earned teaching elocution when she was younger), were supported by my father and his brothers. Every fall the two ladies closed the house in Natchez and Hampton drove them down to Anse La Butte in the Cajun country of South Louisiana, where my two bachelor uncles lived, and they spent two or three months there—saving all the money they might have spent on utilities and food. Down there Hampton took on another role. He drove them down, took off his chauffeur's uniform, put on an apron, cooked breakfast, cleaned up the house, cooked dinner, removed his apron, put on his waiter's jacket, set, served, and cleared the table, put his apron back on and washed the dishes. But what I hadn't thought of: Where were his wife and daughter? Did they go down separately to Anse La Butte and find a house and live there during the winter? And where did Hampton *stay?* Nothing about the house suggests that there were separate servants' quarters. My bachelor uncles, like the rest of the people in our world, were suffering from the Depression. The house at Anse La Butte was . . . well . . . almost indescribable.

I simply do not know the answers to these questions. The subject was never mentioned in my hearing. And, in fact, I didn't know until after his death, when I learned that she had come back from St. Louis to Natchez to bury him and settle his estate, that Hampton had a daughter.

But I was telling about 1931, about what happened to Hampton when the old man died and the place was sold.

I begin to try to imagine what a catastrophe it must have been, but I think there is no way I can make myself understand, *feel*, what he must have felt. There was no work anywhere. Daily, tramps who had been millionaires knocked at the doors of white men's houses and black men's cabins and begged for a day's work in exchange for food. In the cities children fought over the contents of garbage cans. Hampton was plunged from being the most successful, most prestigious black man in his world to being threatened with starvation. With being, under the freezing rains of February, thrust out into the ice-encrusted fields that he had managed so carefully, the profits of which he had husbanded so wisely.

It may be that the nephews let him and his wife and daughter stay in their cabin for the time being. But if they needed money, it may have been essential to take action, close the deal. And the new owners may have cleared everyone out. Hampton did not speak to me of any of this, not of his fears for his family or of the old man, his employer, who "kept a close eye on operations," who "saw that the animals were looked after," but who left him nothing. He did not speak of his desperation, his rage.

This is what he told me.

"I went to Natchez," he said. "I went to see the old man's lawyer, Mr. Laub. I had known him for some years, because of course we had always had business with him. Sometimes the old man would go, but sometimes he'd sign what needed to be signed and I would come over, bring the papers. And then, I had some interests of my own that Mr. Laub took care of. But that was later. So, when the nephews sold the place, I thought, before I set out to do what I had already planned, I would call on him. Of course he knew all about what had happened. He'd filed the probate and handled the sale.

" 'What are you going to do, Hamp?' he said to me. 'Where are you going?'

" 'Well, sir,' I said, 'I'm thinking about going to New Orleans, applying down there with the Southern Railroad to be a Pullman porter.' Everybody knew that was the best job Coloreds could get in those days. 'I was going to ask you for a letter of recommendation,' I said.

"He was one of those small Jews," Hampton said to me. "Bald headed. Stocky. He was an educated man— I don't mean just the law. He had gone to school in the East. Soft voiced. I can hear his voice to this day.

"'Don't do it,' he said. 'Don't do it, Hamp. There are colored men down there waiting in line for those jobs, men with recommendations from the best people in New Orleans.'

"'I have to find suitable employment, Mr. Laub,' I said.

"'I know. I know. But let me tell you,' he said, 'there are people sleeping in the streets in New Orleans, people living on take-homes, working, not for money, for *food* . . . You don't know anybody. You might die down there.'

"Well, of course I knew things were bad, but . . . 'I have to find suitable employment,' I said again.

"So he turned his swivel chair around, looked out the window behind his desk, left me sitting there a while and then he turned back.

"'I have a friend,' he said, 'a client. A widow lady who recently lost her chauffeur. I think you would find

her a good person to work for.' He was quiet again for a
few minutes and I didn't say anything either. Then he
said, 'Hamp, I don't think you're going to find anything
better, considering how things are.' Then, 'If you'd like
me to, I can recommend you to her.'

"So I said thank you very much. 'She's Mrs. J. R.
Ayres,' he said, and he called her right then on the telephone and set up an interview for me the next morning."

"When I left his office," Hampton said to me, "I
went out to see my friend Mose Hutton. You knew
Mose, didn't you?"

"By reputation," I said. "I remember hearing my
grandmother speak of him." Mose Hutton was by reputation the finest cabinetmaker in southwest Mississippi.
Everyone who had fine work to be done called on him.

"I stayed overnight with him," Hampton said.
"There was no point in my going back to Louisiana
when I had an interview scheduled with your grandmother the following morning. But I had never heard
of your grandmother. Mainly I wanted to ask Mose if
Mrs. Ayres was a suitable person for me to work for.
Mose knew everybody. Of course," he added, "I didn't
think Mr. Laub would steer me wrong, but after all . . .
I know he was the best lawyer in Natchez, but after all,
he was a Jew."

II

If Mose Hutton had ever seen the house at Anse La Butte where my grandmother and great-aunt spent a couple of months every winter with my bachelor uncles, Doc and Robert, I wonder if he would have told Hampton that Mrs. Ayres was a suitable person to work for. No use to blame the condition of the house or my uncles' choice of circumstances on the Depression. Years later, after the Second World War, when the LaGrange oil field opened up around Natchez and there was enough money coming in from oil pumped on their home property to support my uncles in whatever style they cared for, Doc continued to live as he always had, a solitary man in an old house in the country— only now it was the house he had grown up in.

I keep thinking that this story must be about how little we know each other, how isolated we stay, but then, it may be about eccentricity, about rejection (or loss) of a particular world and choice of another, about outsiders—who they are, how they live, and how they perceive themselves—but . . . I don't know. Maybe there are so many things going on in every life that it's not possible to do more than set down what one knows and let it go at that.

Here's the house at Anse La Butte: a story-and-a-half Southern farmhouse with a steep pitched roof (rusty corrugated tin) and a long porch across the front. It's old—pre–Civil War—hasn't been painted for decades, and appears to be on the verge of collapse. The shutters (a few missing) were meant to open and close —not like fake modern shutters—and some still do. Others sag from broken hinges. Gutters are rigged to direct rainwater into a tank set up on a high platform. Someone has nailed ladderlike steps onto the steep roof (presumably for climbing up to tar over the rusty spots). Everything is weathered to a mottled gray. About three feet off the ground the color of the walls changes, darkens. This is the result of a watermark from an old flood —the area below the watermark must have been repainted. We are in rice country—South Louisiana. The levees controlling the flow of water into and out of the rice fields make the area vulnerable to flash flooding. But this mark indicates that at some time the water stood for a long time. Perhaps it was during the great 1927 flood.

I am looking out the kitchen window now. Across a wide, desolate, swampy field I see an oil derrick—a wooden oil derrick. My uncles have constructed their own derrick, drilled their own well. A Model T Ford sits beside the derrick, one wheel off the ground, resting on a treadmill, which in turn is attached to the rotary table that turns the drilling rig. It takes a long time to drill an oil well (even when oil is close to the surface of the earth) with a Model T engine. Six months to get to eighteen hundred feet, my brother guesses when I ask him. With modern equipment it would take a day. But, however long it takes, the well eventually comes in and is free flowing—four or five barrels a day, enough to buy groceries and shotgun shells and khaki work pants. A pipe is rigged from the well to the house to carry the natural gas that will serve for cooking, heating the water that comes in from the rain tank, and in winter heating the house—all this if a change in pressure doesn't cause an explosion, burn the house down, and kill everybody in it.

A few skinny cows are grazing around the edges of the oil-slicked swamp. Dead trees stand up here and there over the black water.

Here is one of the first stories I remember hearing as a child about my uncles. It happens during the time of year when the two ladies and Hampton are visiting at Anse La Butte. I see my great-aunt, pince-nez firmly in place on her large, high-bridged nose ("Thank God," my mother said from time to time, "none of you children got the Henderson nose"), grizzled hair arranged in an invisible hair net. I seem to recall her voice, charged with excitement as she told the story. And I see

Doc: tall, heavyset, vigorous. His hair is auburn, wavy, his color high. I see his smile. I remember him as a huge, gentle man, almost always smiling, saying, "Eh? Eh?" after he has asked a question or made a statement meant to pull your leg. Robert is slighter, narrow faced, more withdrawn.

In the story it's raining. The rain is not just an ordinary rain, it's a deluge. As the story is told to us, it goes like this: Twenty-four inches in twenty-four hours! The ground is saturated. Water is rising, rising behind the low levees that surround the rice fields. Doc and Robert are somewhere out under the heavy sky, moving their cows to higher ground—perhaps to one of the rice field levees. The Model T? I don't know where it is. My grandmother and great-aunt and Hampton are in the house, anxious, moving from window to window. Water is pouring into the yard from the swampy area beyond the fence. It's raining harder now. The water has surrounded the house and is creeping up on the brick piers that support the porch. The two ladies speak to Hampton of moving furniture to the attic. Where is the green Buick? Hampton must be worried about the Buick. Has he moved it to high ground? Where are Doc and Robert? Has something happened to them? Will the water come into the house? It is surrounded now and water is lapping at the porch.

"Oh, we were so frightened," my great-aunt says. "Hampton, remember how frightened we were?"

Perhaps we're at dinner when she tells this tale, in my grandmother's house in Natchez, seated in the dining room at the long, elegantly set Chippendale table. Hampton has cleared the dinner plates away and set finger bowls in their place. He laughs indulgently. "Yes, Miss Corinne," he says.

"But here they come," my aunt says. "At first we could barely see them for the rain. They're wading across the field, water up over their knees. But they're safe! They're pulling a boat—a pirogue—and if the water comes into the house, they can take us out. We were so relieved!" she says. "Remember, Hampton? They were all right. Now everything would be all right."

"They had on their waders, their hip boots," my grandmother says softly.

"Here they came," my aunt says. "It was dark, almost like night, the rain was so heavy. And we ran out on the porch to greet them and they came groping up the steps and . . ." She looks at us slyly. Her stories always have a proper ending.

"First Doc," she says. "The rain pouring, and the water—you can almost see it rising. Your Uncle Doc looks out over the fields, water as far as you can see. 'Quite a shower,' he says. 'Quite a shower.'"

"'Oh, boys,' Sister says. 'Boys.' (Didn't you, Sister?) 'Where have you been? We've been so worried.'

"And Doc takes off his hat and shakes it. 'Wet,' he says. 'Eh? Eh? Cows were getting wet.'

"Robert is right behind him. He ties the pirogue to a post and takes off his hat and shakes it. 'Quite a shower,' he says. 'Quite a shower.'"

III

After their mother and aunt grew old and feeble and needed live-in help, Doc and Robert moved to Natchez and lived with them. And when the two old ladies died, Doc moved to the country to the farm his father and grandfather had owned, the house he had grown up in. There he looked after his cows, listened to the singsong whine of a pumping oil well (this one drilled by an oil company that paid him royalties), and counted the cycles. (Although most people don't know it, the amount of oil produced by a pumping well can be calculated by measuring the length of the pump's stroke and counting the number of strokes per minute. If you do know this fact, you can make sure that the oil company which drilled your well and pays you royalties is not cheating you.) Robert, too, counted cycles and looked after cows; but after a while he began to look around him, and at last he married, late, the widow of a cousin, and his style began to be influenced by his wife's preferences. In fact, he moved into her house in town, began to enjoy parties, and got to be quite a dandy.

As for my grandmother's house in town, after the two ladies died and the furniture and silver and household effects had been divided among the brothers, per the specifications in the two wills, the brothers put the house on the market. They had not thought there would be much difficulty selling it—it was an 1840s town house, and Natchez was already a tourist town—but they were wrong. The house had been wired for electricity in the twenties and plumbed for natural gas in the early thirties, but except for the installation of a telephone, which my grandmother distrusted (she warned us repeatedly that it might electrocute us and answered its ring with an interrogative "Well?" as if asking the instrument to account for itself), there had been no other innovations since 1900. A buyer would have to invest considerable money in improvements. It was also the case that the real estate market was in one of its periodic slumps. The house did not sell. Some months passed. The brothers lowered the asking price twice, and then reduced it below the assessed value. At last Hampton intervened.

"If people thought I went with the house," he said

to my father one day, "I think they would find it more interesting."

"Well," my father said. "Well. Hmm." He didn't say yes, probably because he thought such a suggestion was ridiculous and he didn't want to hurt Hampton's feelings. But he didn't say no, because there was always the chance that Hampton was right.

Two weeks later the house sold.

Afterwards my cousin Kathie told me she had run into Hampton at the bank one day and told him that she'd heard the Ayres house had sold.

"Yes," he said. "It has, Miss Kathie."

"Well," she said, "I heard from the folks who bought it that you're going to continue to work for them." Hampton, she told me, looked at her as if she were insane.

"No, no, Miss Kathie," he said. "Indeed not. Perhaps they misunderstood something I said. I'm retiring. It's time for me to retire. And besides . . ." He lowered his voice. "Those people are Jews."

My ex-husband, the father of my children, is Jewish. That is, although he is not a religious man, his mother was Jewish and under Jewish law he is a Jew. I remember now how, after Hampton was in the nursing home, I was made uncomfortable by his loud, penetrating voice when he was telling me about his life. Was it in the nursing home that he said of his lawyer and adviser, Mr. Laub, "After all, he was a Jew"? Probably. Probably he made that comment for my benefit, to put me in my place, to give me notice that in his view my status had been irreparably damaged.

IV

*T*here is disagreement in our family about why my grandmother and her sister stayed so long each year during the 1930s at Anse La Butte. My impression from my father was that in this way Doc and Robert, although times were hard and they had barely enough money to feed themselves, managed to share in the responsibility for their support. My mother, however, knew very well that it was my father who covered the rest of the year's expenses and she thought her brothers-in-law should be ashamed of themselves. She would have said that Grandmother took Hampton down every year to clean house for her sons—with the implication that they were too lazy to clean house for themselves. But they weren't lazy. They raised sugarcane and made syrup with their own mill. They looked after their cows. They were mighty hunters: duck and quail and doves and deer, once even a bear, fell to their guns and were brought to their table. They caught bream and bass and crappie and raised goats to barbecue. Above all, it seemed to me, they lived the life they wanted to live. But, in any case, how could you accuse men who built their own oil derrick out of used lumber and split cypress logs, drilled a well with an engine from a Model T Ford, and carried the oil to market in their own pickup truck of being lazy? Something else, something deeper, more threatening, must have been buried beneath my mother's judgment. Perhaps she sensed a weakness in my father because he did not force his brothers to carry a share of the load, feared that we, her children, would suffer because of this weakness. Times were hard. Money was important.

On the other hand, to keep the record straight, I should say that I don't know for a fact that Doc and Robert's well at Anse La Butte produced only four or five barrels of oil a day. I was guessing. Maybe it was twenty or thirty—or a hundred. Is that possible?

I asked my mother once why she thought Doc—so genial, so easygoing, and handsome, too, I thought, in a heavyset country way—had never married. Did he have lady friends, or was he just solitary?

"Oh," she said, "he had a lady friend for quite a long time down in Lafayette, but they never married."

I think now of another story. This one was told to my brother by Jean Broussard, one of Doc's Anse La

Butte friends who drove up to Natchez for his funeral —as did a number of his South Louisiana friends, men who hunted with him and attended the yearly goat barbecue at Anse La Butte.

"I remember the last time I saw Doc," Mr. Broussard said. "Out at Anse La Butte. He was in that house —you know that house?"

My brother laughed. "Yes," he said. "I know that house."

"Eh . . . There he was, sitting there in the living room. Had his feet up on the fireplace fender. Eating a doolie [a doolie is a cold sweet potato]. 'Broussard,' he says,'Broussard! Eh? Come in. Sit down. Sit down. Have a doolie. Let's talk about how the poor folks live.' "

When Doc died, my father, as eldest of the brothers, was his executor. His estate, consisting of the house at Anse La Butte, modest oil royalties from his and Robert's still-producing well, his car, and a share in the royalties and the furniture from the division of my grandmother's estate (the Chippendale dining table had gone to him), was divided among the surviving brothers. Years later, Hampton, sitting in his wheelchair in the nursing home, told me what had happened to the car.

We'd been sitting together in the parlor area of the nursing home. Several of the old people were sitting around, one or two watching television, but most just sitting, slumped in their chairs, staring, occasionally muttering, as distracted and lonely old people often do. One or two were watching us and, it seemed to me, eavesdropping on our conversation. I was uneasy, uncomfortable, for Hampton had been talking to me about his own predicament. He had sold his house, he said, and the small rental house that he owned. He was spending down his life's savings. There was not much money left.

"I ask you," Hampton said. His breathy, nasal voice seemed too loud, penetrating. One of the old ladies muttering to herself in her wheelchair stopped muttering and gazed fixedly at us. I wished he would speak more quietly. "I ask you, what are we going to do when the money's gone? I ask you. What are we going to do?"

I did not know. I had no idea. I did not want to be part of Hampton's "we." I had my own family to think of, my own obligations. But what I said was, "Don't worry about it, Hampton. Put it out of your mind. We'll manage somehow." What I thought was: Well, my brother'll figure something out.

We were both silent, uneasy, for a few minutes. Then Hampton said to me abruptly, "Did I ever tell you about what happened to Mr. Newman's car?" (Newman was my Uncle Doc's name, but no one except Hampton called him by it.)

"No," I said, happy for the change of subject. "I don't think so."

"Your father told you, maybe?"

I shook my head.

"You knew Mr. Newman had a lady friend down in Lafayette?"

My mother, as I've said, once told me that Doc had gone out for a number of years with a lady in Lafayette, but it had not occurred to me that he might still, in his old age, be spoken of as "having a lady friend." He and the lady had not gotten married and, if I'd thought of their romance at all (which I hadn't for years), I would have assumed that after they didn't get married, they parted. Wasn't that the way things used to be back in the twenties, when people either did or didn't get married?

When I had asked my mother years earlier about Doc's solitary life, I had asked about Robert, too.

"Well, you know," she'd said, "Robert courted Kathleen Roberts for at least ten years and then she popped up and married one of the Boltons and that was the end of that. She certainly feathered her nest with more down than Robert Ayres could ever have supplied. As for Doc . . ." She shook her head.

"Well," I said, "but what about Doc?"

My mother is not a part of this story except insofar as she formed me and my view of my father's family. But she must be given weight in making sense of all that I put down here. I am her child. There is no doubt in my mind that she considered my grandmother an enigma, closed off, walled in—a person who lived someplace other than the real world. "Oh, the Hendersons," she would say, "the Hendersons can do no wrong." I think she could say this and mean it both literally and ironically.

"Why didn't they get married?" I said.

"Your grandmother didn't approve of her," my mother said.

"But . . . Why not? Was she a Catholic?"

"Well, that, too," my mother said, "but she just wasn't . . . quite . . . quite . . . She worked for the telephone company."

"An operator!" I said.

"Well, I think, eventually, a supervisor," my mother said. "But even so . . . Your grandmother . . ."

So this is the first part of the story to which Hampton gave me the last part. As for the middle, perhaps we can dream on it and come up with a middle.

"The day after the funeral," Hampton said, "your father called me in and handed me the keys to Mr. Newman's car and told me to take it down to the Buick company and get it completely checked out and washed and greased, new tires put on, if it needed them, and take it down to Lafayette and give it to Miss (I have forgotten the lady's name). So I did. Took it on down there, drove out to her house, knocked at the door. She knew me, of course. I'd seen her sometimes when your grandmother would be staying out at Anse La Butte, and your uncle would send me to town with a message for her.

"'Well, Hamp,' she says, 'how are you? I'm glad to see you.' And I started to tell her about Mr. Ayres sending me with the car, but she interrupted me and said he'd called and she knew I was coming. It was late in the day, almost dark, no bus going back to Natchez until morning. I handed her the keys and turned around to leave, walking, but she called me back. 'There's not a bus out of town tonight, Hamp,' she says. 'Why don't you keep the car until tomorrow morning. Go on, go out, enjoy yourself, bring it back tomorrow and I'll take you to the station.'

"'No, thank you,' I say. 'I'm much obliged, but no thank you.'

"'Have you got any place to stay tonight?' she says. 'I could put you up.'"

"'I've made arrangements,' I say." Hampton had

been leaning forward in his wheelchair, intent on keeping my attention. Now he sat back, rested his hands on his huge, solid belly, and gave me a look that seemed to imply a scorn deeper than he could articulate.

That was the end of the story.

And the middle? Ah, the middle. What happened to the middle?

V

I have written elsewhere of the aborted or perhaps nonexistent plot said to have been concocted in 1861 by slaves in Natchez and Adams County, Mississippi, and of the "trial" that resulted in the torture and execution of some thirty or more of the so-called plotters. There is very little documentation of the proceedings at Cherry Grove Plantation, where some of the slaves were murdered, and almost none of what happened during the interrogations held at the racetrack in the town of Natchez. Some of the "plotters"—the murdered slaves—were house servants, the sons of maids and cooks and seamstresses. Some were "carriage drivers, fancy boys—confidential servants," as one document put it: the chauffeurs and Pullman porters of the antebellum South. Several could read. They were aware of events that field hands perhaps did not hear of. They knew that Mr. Lincoln was coming and they could pass the word along.

John Roy Lynch, future lawyer and United States congressman, was the slave of my great-grandparents, Mr. and Mrs. A. V. Davis of Natchez. He and his mother were house servants and lived in the servants' quarters at Dunleith, the Davises' Natchez home. Mrs. Davis (born Sarah Surget) had taught him to read. She held worship services for the house slaves and taught them hymns. She was concerned for their souls. In his autobiography, written late in life, Lynch recalls a verse from one of the hymns he learned. "To serve the present age, my calling to fulfill. Oh may it all my powers engage to do my master's will." "The impression the teacher endeavored to make upon our youthful minds," Lynch writes, "was that the master referred to was our earthly master, in the person of her husband, Mr. Davis."

Mr. Davis thought Lynch a clever lad, asked him questions, and laughed at his answers. Once, though, in the view of Mrs. Davis, an answer overstepped the bounds of humility. Unfortunately for Lynch, as it seemed at the time—but fortunately, as it turned out— he was sent, because of his "impudence," to work as a field hand on one of the Davises' Louisiana plantations. This happened in 1861. Lynch was therefore not in Natchez when the "uprising" didn't take place and the torture and executions followed. If he had been, he might have been among those murdered by his master and mistress's friends and kinsmen during the examinations at the racetrack in Natchez.

There is no mention in his autobiography of these proceedings: the "trial" of the accused slaves, conducted by "the gentlemen of the neighborhood," or of the deaths of more than thirty of them by hanging or under the whip. But Lynch must have known of these events. His master and mistress were connected by blood or marriage or friendship with every one of the perpetrators.

A slave named Bill Postlethwaite is supposed to have been the head of the group of town Negroes who joined the conspiracy. The only known reference to him is in the diary of a wealthy planter named William Minor, who with his son John was present at the interrogations.

> It was, I thought, clearly proved that there was a plot between a number of negroes on several plantations in the neighborhood of "Second Creek" & negroes in Natchez with a negro named Bill Postlethwaite at their head to rise to murder their master some day this month . . . Bill Postlethwaite thought it would be an easy job now as so many men had gone away . . .

(Gone, that is, to the war. It was September 1861.)

After the Civil War, Minor's daughter-in-law, his son's widow, sued the federal government for restoration of property, on the grounds that her husband had been a federal sympathizer who had attempted to prevent the hangings or at least to lessen the severity of the examinations of the slaves involved in the Second Creek incident.

It seems likely that Postlethwaite was interrogated and executed with the rest, but his fate is unknown.

Postlethwaite, an unusual name, is the surname of A. V. Davis's great-uncle. One deduces that Bill Postlethwaite may have been the slave of one of the Davis-Surget connection.

The dream I have for this story is to find a connection between Bill Postlethwaite and Hampton, between John Roy Lynch and Hampton, but it is highly unlikely that there is any connection to be found in the records, in history, in the real world. The connection, if there is one, must be found elsewhere.

VI

Among the ladies who lived in Autumn Leaves nursing home during the years when Hampton lived there was an elderly cousin of mine named Mary Postlethwaite, one of those village eccentrics every small town has a dozen or so of. In Natchez there was the lady who walked slowly, always looking down, so as not to step on an ant and thereby take a life; and there was the lady who, to avoid contamination, never touched anything or anybody, even her own children, with an ungloved hand; and the kleptomaniac who sometimes wrapped the silver spoons she had purloined while having afternoon tea with an old friend and gave them back to the friend's son or daughter as a wedding present. There was the gentleman who, everyone said, was immensely talented, destined for a career as a concert pianist until he lost a finger in a hunting accident; for the rest of his life he was a recluse, living, together with his goats and chickens, in a house called Goat Castle. And there was the gentleman who could not enter his place of business until he had touched every panel of the front door nor sit down at his desk until he had touched every object on it. Of all these only the concert pianist came to grief. He was accused, briefly, of having murdered his next-door neighbor, an equally eccentric maiden lady, in a quarrel over a trespassing pig. Later, though, he was exonerated. It was decided that the murderer must have been the itinerant black man who was shot to death when he did not stop at a sheriff's posse's command to halt.

And there was my distant cousin Mary Postlethwaite.

Mary's obsession was a not uncommon one. I've read from time to time of other aging people who cannot bear to throw away papers and who live in the shrinking clear spaces of houses where magazines and newspapers are piled ceiling high. They end up sleeping in chairs because all the beds are covered with papers. Thus Cousin Mary.

People like these, of course, are common enough in cities, too, but in small towns in the past, towns where everyone knew everyone else, their idiosyncrasies were perhaps more likely to be made room for. And the eccentrics were less likely to end up in prison or the loony bin.

Mary was intelligent. She had taught herself as a young woman to do research in the county records, and over the years she eked out a small inheritance by tracing land titles and looking up wills in the chancery clerk's office. It was a scant living until the oil strikes at Cranfield and LaGrange in the forties made title searches an essential part of the oil business. Thereafter Mary was in demand—no less eccentric, though.

I remember well the last time I saw her. It must have been on one of those visits to Natchez in the late forties to see my grandmothers. It was fall, a chill in the air, the leaves turning. My cousin Kathie and I, early one evening, driving in from the country, saw Mary, tall, thin, horse faced, wearing a cloche pulled down over her ears and a long-waisted dress that may have been stylish in the 1920s, sitting on the retaining wall in front of the Presbyterian manse. There was a large canvas satchel at her feet. It must have been close on to seven o'clock, already getting dark.

"What do you suppose Mary's doing?" Kathie said. "She's half a mile from home." We drove on a block or so, then, "We'd better go back," Kathie said. We circled the block and pulled up in front of the manse and she got out. "Mary," she said, "Can we give you a lift? Take you home? You remember Josephine, don't you? Laura's daughter. Where are you headed?"

Mary nodded to me. "I'm just bringing these books back to the courthouse," she said. "But I felt a bit weary and I sat down here to rest and admire the manse. It's lovely in the twilight, isn't it? Doesn't look so pink. You know, you never should have painted the bricks that dreadful pink."

"Mary!" Kathie said, "I didn't have anything to do with painting the bricks. I hate that color." She looked at the canvas satchel. "Books," she said. "They look awfully heavy."

"Well," Mary said, "I must admit, Kathie, I was taken

somewhat by surprise. From time to time I've simply taken a few of the ledgers home from the office to search some titles I've been working on   ."

Kathie reached down and pulled out a huge, worn, leather-bound ledger stamped 1850–1860. "Ah," she said. ("My hair simply stood on end when I saw that ledger," she told me afterwards.)

"I work backwards, of course," Mary said. "And I'd gotten back to '60 and . . . well, I did just take these two home to . . . and lo and behold, they decide down there to put the ledgers in order on the shelves (although *I* knew where everything was), but somebody's coming from somewhere to inspect, they say . . Well, of course I hadn't told anybody I . . . So I need to return them before they work back to the fifties. You see? I just thought I'd slip in . . ."

"But Mary," Kathie said, "the courthouse is closed, isn't it? Can't you wait until tomorrow?"

"Oh, I have a key," she said. "Everyone who uses the courthouse has a key."

We took her, as directed, to the side entrance. "I'll help you carry them up," Kathie said.

"No, no. Just leave me. I'll be fine."

"But Mary . . . They're heavy."

"It's just a step to the chancery clerk's office, and the records room," Mary said firmly. "I will be fine, Kathie.

I expect I will be here for a while—working." She smiled at me. "I get so much pleasure out of reading the old records," she said. "Wills especially. I know everything about everybody."

So we left her.

Although I didn't know it, by the time I paid my last call on Hampton, Mary, too, was a resident of Autumn Leaves nursing home. After the last chair in her house was stacked with papers and the hall to the bathroom blocked, she had moved a cot into the chancery clerk's office one night and set it up behind a row of tall cabinets at the back of the records room and begun to sleep there. No one could decide what to do about her. No one had the nerve to ask for her key. But she fell one afternoon, reaching down a heavy ledger from a high shelf, and broke her hip. While she was in the hospital, the city and county officials agreed to have the locks on the courthouse doors changed to protect themselves, in case she should get ambulatory again. But, after all, she didn't. She went directly from the hospital to Autumn Leaves and her house was sold and all those old papers thrown away.

A reporter from the local newspaper, when Cousin Mary had her ninety-fifth birthday, went out to Autumn Leaves to interview her about old times in Natchez. "It doesn't do to outlive all your contemporaries," she said then. "All my friends—my colleagues—are dead. The only person left in Natchez with whom I have anything in common—he's out here, too, in this dreadful place, this staging area, waiting for the ferry to carry us over the Styx—is my cousin Nellie Ayres's chauffeur." This statement was recorded in the reporter's notes, with a question mark beside "Styx" (which she had spelled "Sticks"), but it was not included in the feature story.

VII

*H*ampton had mentioned to me when he was telling me about his youth that the lawyer, Mr. Laub, had handled his "interests" as well as his employer's and, after he died, I was curious enough about these to ask my friend Brent Forman, who was a member of Mr. Laub's firm, if he had ever had any dealings with Hampton. Indeed, yes, Brent said, he had inherited Hampton when Mr. Laub died and had handled his affairs until his death.

"He had a considerable estate when I took him over," Brent said, "but you may know, your brother probably told you (he was Hampton's executor), it was all gone by the time he died. All drained away by those years in the nursing home."

"Yes," I said. "The last time I saw him, Hampton told me the money was almost gone."

"He was worth well over a hundred thousand dollars at one time," Brent said, "but I don't think there was enough left to pay for the funeral."

"A hundred thousand dollars!" I said. "Really?"

"Well, he owned his house, of course, and he had some rental property. But investments, too. He was an interesting man," Brent said. "We used to talk occasionally, when he'd come to see me. Did you know he was an atheist? Or maybe a theologian would classify him as a Zoroastrian. In any case he told me once that only an evil God could have created the world we live in."

I shook my head. "He never talked to me about religion," I said. "I remember, though, that my great-aunt Corinne used to pray for him at dinner. I mean she always said her own extemporaneous blessing, no matter who had blessed the food, and she often asked the Lord to lead Hampton to the church. I suppose I would have thought that he just hadn't bothered to think about . . . about . . . I mean I wouldn't have thought of anything so formally defined as being an atheist. I reckon I never really thought about the significance of my aunt's prayers. She prayed for so many things, and one's attention drifted off.

"But then," I went on, "then, later, I remember, after she was quite old, maybe in the last year or two of her life, I remember her telling me . . . I can just see her. She was so happy she wept and her pince-nez fell off her nose. She told me Hampton had been baptized, had joined the church. And he was in the room when she told me. I don't remember what he said, though. I just remember him smiling that reserved, condescending smile."

Afterwards I couldn't stop thinking about what Brent had told me: *Only an evil God could have created the world we live in.*

It occurred to me that Hampton might have told my aunt that he had joined the church so that she would stop pestering him. A different sort of man might really have joined a church and paid lip service to religion to keep her and anybody else, black or white, from persisting in trying to convert him. But not Hampton. I can believe, though, that he might have considered the matter deeply and converted to Christianity. I can even believe that he joined a church in order to ensure that he would have a suitable funeral service and burial. But . . .

Only an evil God could have created the world we live in.

I ask myself what I missed in Hampton's life, what led him to this awful conclusion: God is not simply mysterious, unfathomable, not even indifferent, but, if He exists, He is evil.

Sometimes, in the night, I wake up hearing his voice. He is speaking to his lawyer, his peer—to Brent, Mr. Laub's successor—saying those words.

Oₙ Second Creek

"It was written I should be loyal to the nightmare of my choice."

—Joseph Conrad, *Heart of Darkness*

Second Creek

IN MAY OF 1861 there happened (or did not happen) in southern Adams County, Mississippi, a conversation among the slaves of several planters who lived along the banks of Second Creek. The talk, if it occurred, concerned a projected uprising to coincide with the imminent coming of Mr. Lincoln and the Yankees. The slaves would kill the masters and "ride the ladies." Such a conversation, under the laws of the time, was felonious and punishable by death. Later, someone named Benny may have reported hearing—or over-hearing—this conversation to someone in the white community. Benny, called by two of the slaves "Mas' [Master] Benny," seems to be the only link between these slaves' words and their masters' actions.

There were no legal arrests, no trials, no testimony,

so far as the records show, by Benny or any other white person. But in September and October of the same year a number of these slaves were questioned and thirty or more were executed by a committee of "the gentlemen of the neighborhood." All, it appears, were examined under the whip, some, it may be, tortured in other ways, to extract accounts of this "plot." There is no record of the burial place of those executed. No newspaper recorded these events.

A man named Lemuel Conner was "president" of at least a part of the proceedings and kept notes, which his family preserved and eventually gave, along with other family papers, to the archives at Louisiana State University. Some years ago, the historian Winthrop Jordan came upon the notes by chance during research on another project, and he has written a book speculating about the nature of these events and nonevents called *Tumult and Silence at Second Creek.*

Second Creek wanders through Adams County from northeast to southwest and flows first into the Homochitto River and then into the Mississippi. My family has owned a farm on the north end of the creek for nearly two hundred years. My son and his family live there today, and so Jordan's book cannot but be peculiarly interesting to me.

I am a writer of fiction, but the record that I begin

today, like Jordan's book, like all history and all fiction, is a tangle of truth and lies, facts and purported facts, imaginary and real events. History, it's been said more than once, is written by the winners. But of some contests even the winners may be loathe to leave a record.

1995: Liza Conner Martin

*T*he house, a one-story 1930s cottage, needed painting and repairs—white shreds peeling off the clapboard, gutters sagging, the yard ill-kept. A huge cherry-laurel tree clawed at the front window on the left; an ancient cedar, riven by the last ice storm, dragged the ground on the right. Going in, even in company with my large, calm, gentle-voiced cousin, I was afraid I might not be able to make Liza understand who I was, much less persuade her to answer my questions—if she had answers. She was ninety-nine years old, stone deaf and half-blind, but she was still alert and welcomed company, Kathie had told me. We would print our questions and our answers to her questions in large letters with black Magic Markers on the legal-sized pads we carried.

She would be glad to see us, Kathie said, and would know who I was as soon as I wrote, RICHARDSON'S DAUGHTER. My father was her third cousin.

A black woman met us at the door. She'd answered

the phone when Kathie had called to ask permission to come—had refused the first day, saying that Liza was asleep, but today: "Come on then, she's awake and feeling pretty good. She might stay awake until you get here," she said, "but she sleeps a lot. More and more."

Now Kathie said hello and introduced me, and then: "How are you holding out, Josephine?"

"Thirty years," the black woman said. "I'm tired." Her face was expressionless, my sense of her one of— what? Hostility's too strong. Utter detachment.

"I won't be holding out much longer," she said.

"This is my cousin, Mrs. Haxton," Kathie said. "She's a cousin of Liza's, too. And she's named Josephine—like you."

The black woman looked at me, nodded, stepped back to let us in, turned away, and disappeared. She didn't care whether we came or went.

Liza was lying propped high on a hospital bed, the furniture pushed back to accommodate it—a massive four-poster shoved against one wall, bureaus and chairs arranged to make room for the walker and portable toilet that stood to hand. The four-poster, the small cabinet beside it, the bureau, and every chair—all were piled with magazines, papers, books, scattered snapshots, spiral notebooks, empty envelopes, the mantel above the old sealed-up fireplace crowded with framed photographs and more papers.

"Remember, she can't hear a word," Kathie said, and then, "Hello, Liza," smiling, nodding, bending to kiss her pale forehead.

"My God," I whispered, "she's beautiful. Her skin . . ." I hadn't seen Liza for twenty years, and then only at a couple of family funerals where I was absorbed in my own emotions, and once when I came calling with my mother after Liza's mother's death and found her distracted, dismantling the house before it was sold. I had paid little attention to her dark olive-skinned good looks. Now her hair was white, her skin pale and as unblemished as a child's, as softly wrinkled as you might expect it to be at sixty-five, not a hundred. She looked old, of course, but—I don't know—serene, unused, maybe, no sun spots (liver spots, we used to call them) on her hands and arms, her eyes clear and bright, not milky as old eyes usually are.

Kathie was scribbling on her yellow legal pad and now she held it up, pointed to me: JOSEPHINE— RICHARDSON'S DAUGHTER. IN TOWN A FEW DAYS.

My fiction was that this was a courtesy call, no more. After Liza knew me and felt reassured, then I might ask my questions.

"Write big," Kathie said to me.

I held up my pad. GLAD TO SEE YOU. I'd already printed it on the first page. LAST TIME WAS—I THINK—GRANDMOTHER'S FUNERAL. NELLIE AYRES—HENDERSON, SHE WAS. In this town, this curious pocket of inbred relationships, one might more easily identify oneself with the maiden name of a grandmother than with the name of the unknown outlander one might have married.

Liza frowned, shook her head, then nodded. "Cousin Nellie. Yes," she said. "She died in '52, didn't she? The year before . . . You . . . Let's see, where do you live now? Who'd you marry?"

JACKSON, I wrote. I didn't write that I was divorced. GREENVILLE MAN. KENNETH HAXTON. I flipped a page. On page two I had written, I REMEMBER YOUR MAMA—COUSIN MARY—SO WELL.

She looked at me, puzzled, unbelieving. "You never lived in Natchez and Mama's been dead forty years," she said.

SO WELL. I underlined the words, smiled, flipped the page, held up the pad. WHEN I WAS A LITTLE GIRL VISITING. FAIRY PATHS IN THE GARDEN. STORIES. SHINY STONES. CHINA.

It took her a few minutes to make this out, lips moving.

Kathie glanced at my pad, scribbled, ME TOO. USED

TO TELL US STORIES. And, to me, "Yes, the paths in the garden where the fairies walked. She outlined them with chips of glass and broken china. I hadn't thought of that for years."

"Ah, Mama," Liza said finally. "She was a charmer, wasn't she? Children loved her. Imagination. What an imagination she had. She could keep us listening to stories . . . There she is"—pointing to the mantelpiece— "there in, let's see, in her Pilgrimage costume, isn't she? She loved the excitement, the tableaux, dressing up, make-believe." She shook her head. "Your generation . . . women now." She looked at Kathie. "She'd have been a famous actress."

I crossed the room to the mantelpiece to look at the photograph of a plump elderly woman in black antebellum costume, hoop-skirted, a lace cap on her hair, a too sweet smile on her face.

"I know where everybody is," Liza said. "I *see* them. Bring Mama here." She took the photograph from me and picked up a magnifying glass from the bedside table to examine it.

It crossed my mind that I'd had as a child the vague sense that Cousin Mary was considered a poseur, regarded with tolerant contempt by serious people. But then who were the serious people? Preachers? Presiding Elders? The Women's Auxiliary? And I thought about her husband's knowledge—about what I had come to find out. For he had known, hadn't he? It had been his father who had been present, had kept the record, had preserved it for all those years. But it was not yet time to ask. I flipped a page of my pad and wrote hastily (this would be part of establishing my bona fides as an unthreatening insider), YOUR MOTHER AND MY FATHER'S AUNT ANNA WERE FIRST COUSINS, WEREN'T THEY? FRIENDS?

But this scarcely interested her. "Cousins," she said. "Cousins. I'm not sure." And although another day I might have been curious about her memories of my great-aunt's character (she was a recluse and an eccentric), today I had my mind on other matters.

And so did Liza. She wanted to talk of her own family. She pointed to and named the pictures of her son and his grown children. "I'm a great-grandmother," she said. "Depressing." And then, to Kathie, "There is a letter and an article on the bed there that I want you to see. Right there in that stack on the far side." I've forgotten what she said the letter contained and who it was from. Kathie looked for it in the piles of papers, and then Liza called in the black woman. Whatever it was, it couldn't be found.

"But I was sure it was on the bed," Liza said, and then, "Oh, Kathie, look. Just look. All this stuff. The pictures. All the papers. Already, I'm losing everything, and I'm still alive. What's to become of it when I die?"

"It's precious, all of it," Kathie said softly, and then, recalling herself, wrote, PRECIOUS. VALUABLE. WON'T GET THROWN AWAY. ARCHIVES.

This was my chance. I flipped over a couple of pages on my pad—more family questions I could omit. I had a page that read: I'VE SEEN SOME CONNER PAPERS AT LSU. INTERESTING! Above this I wrote, LEAVE PAPERS TO LSU. ARCHIVES.

For the first time she looked vague, uncomprehending. She was still holding the photograph of her mother and now she laid the magnifying glass on the bedside table and handed the picture to Kathie. "What?"

I underlined LSU AND CONNER PAPERS. YOU GAVE THEM? I wrote hastily.

"Oh." She frowned and thought. "It must have been . . . Yes, they're there. We sent some of them down there a long time ago—going back to, oh, 1800 probably. But here . . . you see . . ."—gesturing to the bed and the bureau—"Grandpa's letters, Mama and Daddy's and mine . . . at the time those still seemed too personal, too close. But now, so many years have gone by, it's more like we're all characters, we're history." She laughed. "Monuments," she said. "You know how far back our families go. We've all been here together since the beginning. Seventeen eighty? Seventeen ninety? Earlier? Of course none of us were here when the

Natchez massacred the French. When was that? Seventeen thirty-something. And then, of course the French came back and massacred the Natchez. But by 1790 . . . Yes. It was when Mama died that we sent . . . And now I still have all these papers, this accumulation. Who's going to straighten it out?"

I WANTED TO ASK YOU, I wrote, ABOUT PAPERS AT LSU. YOUR FATHER, DID HE? . . .

"Ah, Daddy," she said. "Bring me his picture, Kathie. So handsome. Charming. We adored Daddy."

HE WAS LEMUEL CONNER JR.? HIS FATHER LEMUEL, TOO? I wrote.

I have been debating how to make it clear, to put you on notice, so to speak, that every single detail of my story is not true. On the one hand I want you to get a sense of how I approached Liza, how she responded, what the house was like. Her surroundings. But I couldn't take notes and I don't always recall our precise words. Even the geography and the look of the house have faded a little in my memory. It's not that I wish to mislead you. The details I fill in with—the riven cedar tree, the clawing laurel by the front window—these may be substitutes for details I've forgotten, but I'll try to give you as accurately as I can my sense of the way the interview went, where it took place, who we were.

She was not interested in Lemuel Sr. "That's what I mean," she said. "He's so far back. When was he born? Eighteen twenty-something. But Daddy—he wrote a wonderful letter," she said. "I have all his letters to me when I was in college."

IN PAPERS AT LSU, I WAS SO INTERESTED (this was already printed on my pad) IN YOUR GRANDFATHER—LEM SR.'S—ACCOUNT OF THE SLAVE UPRISING IN NATCHEZ IN 1861. DID HE EVER MENTION TO YOU? I added, OR YOUR MAMA? OR DADDY? DID THEY?

She read carefully, shaking her head, doubtful. "No . . . Not something that . . . I don't think . . . And Mama? No . . . no." We never talked about . . ."

IT'S ALL IN THE PAPERS, I wrote hastily. PRECIOUS HISTORICAL DATA. LSU. SLAVE UPRISING. HE WROTE ACCOUNT OF TRIAL. DO YOU REMEMBER? DID YOU EVER SEE MANUSCRIPT?

"Oh, yes, I knew about that," she said calmly, not, I particularly recall, as if it were important or even interesting to communicate to me or anyone her knowledge of the so-called trial, or of what anyone had said about Lemuel Conner's account. More as if the account and its location were to be taken for granted, as one might say about an event—a historical fact or myth: "Those are the Aaron Burr Oaks where Burr was tried." (Aaron Burr was apprehended in Washington, Mississippi, near Natchez.

There are or used to be two trees under which he is supposed to have been "tried" for treason, although he was, of course, tried in Richmond). Or: "That's the hatchet George Washington used to cut down the cherry tree."

"That's where he kept it," she said. She was propped high on her pillows, white hair against white pillowcase, a picture, with her smooth, scarcely crumpled skin and bright, dark eyes that saw so little. She pointed now, the sleeve of her gown falling back from her pale arm, to the small cabinet, veneered in flame-grained mahogany, a door in the front, one small drawer above, that stood beside the four-poster. "There," she said. "It was always right there in the cabinet by their bed. In the old house, I mean, in Mama and Daddy's room. That was their bed. Of course I remember it."

DID YOU EVER READ? . . .

"Can't remember . . . Probably not. But Daddy," she said. She held up the picture that Kathie had handed her. "I wanted to tell you about Daddy. What a fine, fine man he was. And now nobody remembers him. Nobody but me. Not my grandchildren. He was long dead when they were born." And then, "Never mind, never mind," she said. "Something else . . . It was when Josephine said you were coming by, Kathie, I was thinking . . . something I wanted to show you. Papers . . ." She called the sitter in again. "Where are those papers I wanted to show Kathie, Josephine?" she said. "You know. Didn't we put them? . . ."

Josephine raised both hands, mimed bewilderment, pointed at the bed, shook her head. "I already looked, Miss Liza," she said in a normal voice. She turned away, vanished again into the back of the house.

LEDGERS, Kathie wrote. REMEMBER, A WHILE BACK YOU WERE LOOKING FOR A MISSING LEDGER. CHILDREN'S HOME RECORDS.

"No, no, it wasn't that. Oh!" She touched her white cheeks with her white hand, shook her head angrily, seemed ready to clutch at her white hair. "Oh, it makes me so angry, oh, it's so frustrating. Not to be able to read my own papers. Not to be able to sort them out."

The fan turned and turned, lifted and gently rustled the papers on the bed.

"I get so sick of television. Shadows, nothing but shadows. What are they doing? What are they saying? And there are books I'd like to read again. The Bible. I can't even read the Bible."

I scribbled on my pad: LARGE PRINT BOOKS? LIBRARY HAS THEM.

"Yes. Kathie, you could get . . . Do you think you could get a copy . . . Yes, I'd love to reread—maybe that novel by Stark Young. Woodville, you know."

Kathie nodded.

SO RED THE ROSE, I wrote.

"Or a murder mystery, maybe? But I was telling you about Daddy." She picked up his photograph and examined it with the glass. "Put it back where it was," she said. "I know where everyone sits. There at the far end, that's my son and his family. Taken . . . How long ago?"

ABOUT PAPERS, I wrote, SLAVE REVOLT. CAN'T FIND ANYONE WHO'S HEARD OF IT BUT YOU. This was the important question. DID YOUR DADDY TELL YOU WHAT HIS FATHER SAID ABOUT ALL THAT?

She read and pushed the pad away. "No, no," she said. "Just the papers in the cabinet. Mama always said not to throw them away."

"But now . . ." I said (I forgot to write), "isn't there anything you remember that he . . ."

"Mama never threw anything away," she said. "All that broken glass and china made paths for fairies. And now—look at me."

1958: Gold Smith Sr.

Gold and I did not know each other very well, ever. I knew him only as a bard. He used to come to the house, when we would be down in Adams County visiting, and tell us stories. I hear him telling another strange tale, looking at me, a smile of complicity on his face, his eyes questioning. But past that I never knew him. It was my father he cared about. They'd known each other a long time, had hunted together and worked together over the years. "I can see him now," I hear Gold saying tenderly, the first time I saw him after Father died. "The Elder." He always called my devout Presbyterian father The Elder. "Here he comes up on the porch. Sets a while with me. We talk about the fences. Edna fixes us a pitcher of lemonade and a plate of gingersnaps. He was partial to Edna's gingersnaps." It's as if with his voice, with his wife's gingersnaps, Gold blesses the memory of my father.

But I was a different matter. I was, after all, a youngish white woman whom he'd not known as a child and he was an old black man. The year we got acquainted was 1958.

"So . . . You live in the Delta?" Gold says. "Greenville. Yeah—I lived in the Delta one year. Down on Lake Washington. Mr. Lord's place. You know Mr. Lord? Hmmm. But he's probably dead by now. Time when we lived up there, 'twas right after the kaiser blew the whistle and I come back from the war. That was the first war, the one your daddy was in. I'm younger than your daddy. We were both in that war, but I didn't know him then. So, when I come home, I got married

and went to sharecropping with Mr. Lord up in the
Delta, not far from Rolling Fork, Glen Allen, Panther
Burn. That must have been 1919, 1920, before you were
born. Mmm? Well . . . Well, I didn't have no experi-
ence of the Delta. Grew up in Adams County on Second Creek, south end of Second Creek. Poor sandy hill
land, gullies washed everywhere—not much count for
farming. Going back to pine trees and some folks kept
cows. You know Ingle Washington? Ingle, his daddy
kept cows, you know. He was crazy about cows. And
later little Ingle was, too.

"So I went up there and got a crop with him. Mr.
Lord. Me and Edna. Moved into a no-count shack on
his place and he give me thirty acres. I had a mule and
a wagon my daddy had give me. That's what we come
up there in.

"The Delta.

"Soon as I got the cotton land broke up, I commenced to work a nice plot of ground right near the
house where Edna could see to the garden while I was
putting in the crop.

"So Mr. Lord, he rode by one day on his horse.
This was before the people had cars, you know. 'Well,
Gold,' he says, 'I see you settled in.'

"I say, yes, sir. Say I'm putting us in a garden. About
an acre or so.

"'An acre!' he says. 'An acre for a garden? You mean for corn, I reckon. For the mule.'

"'No,' I say. 'I got another spot over there for corn.'

"'Oh,' he says.

"'I figure on greens here,' I say. 'Okra. Tomatoes. Like that. A half acre for sweet potatoes.'

"'What?' he says, like he never heard of sweet potatoes.

"'We're partial to sweet potatoes,' I say.

"'I reckon you are.' He shook his head and just rode on off, but I heard him talking to his horse. 'Half an acre for sweet potatoes,' he says. 'Half an acre.'

"Well, I wondered about that.

"So, come fall. Frost. Me and Edna have done canned a hundred quarts of tomatoes and eat all we could and throwed out bushels. Canned butter beans, string beans. Got plenty black-eyed peas and cowpeas sacked up. I commenced digging sweet potatoes.

"Later on when I come to know your daddy, I told him . . . Hmmph. The Delta. I told him about digging them sweet potatoes. 'On my word,' I say, 'them potatoes was so big we had to cut 'em up with an ax.'

"'Gold!' he says. 'Ha!' You know how he laughs. You can hear him fur as from here to the barn. But it's the gospel truth.

"Well. So it comes time to settle up. I see him down

to the commissary—Mr. Lord, I mean. And he tells me to come on up to the house and get me and Edna's share. 'Bring a bushel basket,' he says. 'You got a bushel basket, ain't you?'

"'A basket,' Edna says when I got home. 'What's he gonna put in a basket?' And 'I don't want none of his basket.'

"Well, I took and got one anyhow, and went on up to his house. Rode my mule—his house was a couple of miles down the road from where me and Edna were cropping and, in fact, I hadn't never been inside his house or paid no attention to it.

"So I ride up there, tie my mule by the watering trough. He's got a big old green turtle swimming in the watering trough, gonna make cooter soup, I reckon. I go up on the back porch and knock at the door. Mrs. Lord, she comes to the door. She knows me. She's seen me more than once at the commissary.

"'Gold,' she says. 'You come to settle up.'

"'Yes'm.'

"'Well, take off your shoes,' she says.

"That set me back. I hadn't ever had no white lady tell me to take my shoes off before I could come in her house.

"So I look down. My feet look clean enough. And I look at her feet and she's got on bedroom slippers.

"She says again, 'Take off your shoes, Gold. You can leave 'em on the porch.'

"So I did. And I come on through the kitchen with my lip poked out, thinking about Edna and my clean shoes, and I'm in the hall, big, wide hall down the middle of the house, and—I told your daddy afterwards, I told him—I couldn't believe my eyes. The floors—the floors was made of plush. Mr. Lord himself, when I got into his office where he was, fixing to settle up, Mr. Lord himself, he didn't have on no shoes. Sock feet sunk up to the ankles in plush.

"The Delta.

"'Where's your basket, Gold?' he says, and I notice he's got a big soup ladle in his hand and there's a open barrel setting by his desk. So I hand him the basket ('twas a peck, though, not a bushel) and he sets it on the floor and commence to ladle money into it out of the barrel. Silver dollars. Measured 'em out by the ladleful until finally he says, 'Well, that's it, Gold,' and I say, 'Yessir.'

"So I carried the basket on home and Edna and me counted the money, counted the dollars. Fifteen hundred and thirty-two silver dollars—and keep—that's what we made cropping for Mr. Lord one year in the Delta—1921.

"The people said to me afterwards that he didn't

never keep no records, so he would always settle up that way—in cash—by the ladleful. Bad years, I reckon, there wouldn't be no ladle, just accounts due at the commissary—and your crop lost.

"But me and Edna didn't care for the Delta. Took that fifteen hundred dollars and come on back to Adams County and bought a piece of land. Raised cattle. By and by we bought another piece. That's when I begun to get to know your daddy and your uncles. I'd work by the day for them sometimes—mostly fences. Split locust posts and mend fences. Hunt with them, too, in the fall. There were plenty quail on the place then. And Edna, she made some money in those days raising turkeys. Of course, she was teaching school, too. She'd gone up to Alcorn College to school a year, and she had her teacher's certificate. Edna was always one for records. She didn't put no faith in ladles full of money."

Gold, Another Day, Another Year

"*I* have done told you this story before. About the white man and his wife and little girl that come to be living back in the Bottom during of the Depression and how I was hunting back in there one day and come on them living in a tent in a clearing and how his wife had this beautiful hair, golden hair, like ropes of gold, down to her waist, and how that man put my hand on her head, his wife's head. 'You want to touch her hair?' he says. 'Hadn't she got the most beautiful hair you ever seen?' And how I said, 'Mister, I wouldn't touch her hair unless you took my hand and laid it on her head,' and how he did—took my hand and laid it on her head. I told you about that.

"But the rest of that story," I hear Gold say, "the rest of that story, when you wrote it down for a book, *you* made it up. Had nothing to do with me. You wrote that I thought he mistook me for a white man. But I ain't no Fleming or no Dinelli that somebody might mistake for a white man. Although, true, my skin is lightish. I got white blood, Indian blood. But I never had a white grandfather left me and my brother six hundred acres of land like you've got in your story. And I never did know much about that white man—as to whether he was a preacher or a labor organizer or a teacher or something else, I never did know. He was a silent fellow. Kept his mouth shut. All I know about him is this."

"*T*here he was," Gold says, "that white man I told you about, back in the Homochitto Bottom in a tent. Got it floored with boards from a fallen-down house in that clearing. A *tent!* It's winter. An old piece of a pickup truck. A wife. A little girl. It was what—'34?

Nineteen thirty-four, '35. The Depression. The schools closed six months that year. I mean our schools, colored schools. So Edna lost three months' salary. (Twenty-five dollars a month she was making.) But these white people, they were worse off than us. I took 'em more than one mess of greens. Took 'em fatback when we killed a hog. Sweet potatoes.

"But here's what I mainly remember about him. He'd come down to the store and when the people come in talking about this and that, he would look at their papers, read their papers, tell them what to do."

"What kind of papers, Gold?" I said. "What are you talking about?"

"You know," he said. He looked at me. That look he had, alert, calculating, waiting, smiling at a secret joke. "A lot of the people then," he said, "they couldn't read the papers, you know."

What was he talking about? Wills? Deeds? Welfare? Pensions? I didn't want to ask again, to break into the train of his narrative. Besides, I didn't know what to ask and I didn't want to seem stupid.

"Later on," he said, "seemed like it wasn't such a good idea setting there in front of the store explaining the papers. At that time there was a dance hall, call it a juke joint, over on the Palestine Road where the people would go to dance on Saturday night. And so he'd go over there and set there and listen to the music (I reckon) and watch the people dance. A white man. And the people would bring him their papers and he'd tell them what they needed to know. And when the weather got better—spring—he'd go to town and be out on the yard there by the courthouse or sometimes over on Franklin Street, if anybody needed him."

"But what did he *do,* Gold?" I said. "I don't understand."

"He'd help the people," Gold said. "Help the people with their papers. And then one day (You got this part all wrong. He wasn't killed like you wrote. You just put that in to make a story, didn't you?) one day him and his wife and little girl, they loaded up their traps in the pickup truck—pots and pans and blankets and fishing poles and baby dolls—and rode on off and I never saw none of them again. Never. Never knew who he was, where he come from, where he went. He didn't say and I didn't ask. That's the true story and that's the way I told it to you. And all these years, I've wondered . . . I've wondered. And nobody but me probably remembers now how he come that winter and helped the people and wasn't afraid and then was gone."

· · ·

1995: Portraits

With regard to ancestors one has few choices. They're back there. One can remember or forget them, investigate or let lie, lie or speak what may perhaps be the truth about them. Of the more recent ones there may exist portraits, letters, diaries, perhaps ambrotypes and photographs. Further back, things are considerably vaguer. I've read that a third of the people of Europe and North America are descended from Charlemagne—he had nineteen children by his four wives and five mistresses. And presumably the other two-thirds of us are descended from other distinguished folk, as well as from assorted serfs and yeomen. My own line from Charlemagne, for example, is said to come through Robert the Bruce, whose descendants somehow get entangled along the way with other Scots named Dunbar, or maybe it was Henderson. You should remember these names. I'll come back to them.

It should be perfectly clear to anyone that I have no control over the character of Charlemagne. I take no responsibility for him, either for his defeats or for his victories, although I applaud his interest in reform of the legal code and in literacy, and wonder why he felt obliged to massacre—put to the sword—forty-five hundred Saxons after their defeat at Verden. His slaughters, like the slaughters of Vlad the Impaler and unlike the Holocaust, seem unreal to me. As a real ancestor, he doesn't interest me. I don't even claim him. Because, of course, as soon as you begin to think about why a third of the people of the Western world are descended from Charlemagne, you realize that, given the human population explosion of the last thousand years, everybody is descended from just about everybody. After all, there were only a limited number of people in Europe in Charlemagne's time, and eventually all their descendants ended up marrying or cohabiting with one another. Who knows, we may also be descended from Vlad, although there were more people in Europe when he lived, and his corner of Europe—Transylvania—was more isolated.

A cousin of mine, in her application for admission to the Colonial Dames, traced her line back to John Quincy Adams's great-grandfather. "And of course," she added in her résumé, "Adams has the honor of being the oldest human name." You see where snobbery can lead.

On the scientific rather than the mythological side, there is that distinguished cave lady who, according to some anthropologist or other, is the true Eve. DNA evidence (don't ask me where it came from) indicates that she is the mother of the entire *Homo sapiens sapiens* subspecies. You notice I exclude *Homo neanderthalensis*. I don't much care for those chinless beetle-browed faces, those squat Venuses with their pendulous breasts—even though I know that recent research indicates they were brainier than Cro-Magnon.

Nobody now, though, has a portrait of our DNA Eve on the dining room wall, any more than a portrait of Charlemagne. What would it look like? Maybe an enlargement, framed in gold leaf, of that lovely intricate double-helix protein chain.

But in Southern families like mine—or New England or other lethargic stay-put clans—where for reasons of poverty, stoicism, self-satisfaction, low blood pressure, or plantar warts, people have avoided moving about, have been content to sit with their feet cocked up or to circle slowly in one small backwater for six or seven generations, in families like these, there are portraits on the walls, papers in the attic. *These* ancestors one relates to in a very different way. One doesn't take credit for Charlemagne or Vlad or Adam and Eve. But these? There they are on one's grandmother's dining room walls. One is presented with them from birth. They look down on the thousand Sunday dinners of childhood. Here are a few of mine.

This one—he's a Henderson—in his decent black

frock coat, looks like a clerk in a Dickens novel. A devout Presbyterian, he was a founder of his church in the Mississippi Territory and author of a book called *Paine Detected*—not a whodunit, a treatise on Thomas Paine's atheism.

Here is a ringletted lady, stern and long faced, looking like a preacher with a wig on, whom, as I know from discarded canvases in the attic, the painter tried to capture three times before she was pleased with the likeness—I draw conclusions about vanity here.

Another lady, wearing wire-framed spectacles, peers at me nearsightedly, a protective hand raised to cover her mouth—I know she's nearsighted because my grandmother remembered her and because my brother and I both inherited that gene through our father. I must also have inherited the gene that made her (so my grandmother told me) almost pathologically shy. She once fell down and broke her glasses hiding in the horse lot from unexpected callers.

Here is a great-grandmother, born in 1820 who lived until 1910. She is caught in a late photograph, her severely tragic mask bearing witness to her life. Homely in her youth, she nevertheless married well, bore twelve children, buried seven. In her prime she had served her community as official layer-out of all those dead whom her doctor husband could not save, including her own children. In her last years, senile, she liked to play dolls with her black keeper.

This fellow, named Dunbar (you'll hear more of him later), was the child of the inappropriate second marriage of a Scottish laird. He emigrated to the new world in the mid-eighteenth century and, like Faulkner's Sutpen, went off to the Caribbean as a young man and brought back the slaves who made his fortune. He distinguished himself as a naturalist, surveyor, and inventor (of the cotton bale), and made a great deal of money from slave-raised cotton and slave-split barrel staves. He was painted early on in the red coat of a British army officer's uniform; but when the Congress gentlemen came down the Mississippi River, he must have commissioned a local artist to cover the red coat with sober civilian black (as the family discovered when the portrait was cleaned in the 1930s). He led the survey of the boundaries of West Florida for the Spanish and of the Red River region for President Jefferson. He wrote to his wife, Diana, in a letter my mother still possessed, "We shall endeavor, my Dearest, to convert these gloomy woods into enchanting bowers and delightful walks." As you can see, he must have been quite unlike Sutpen in many ways.

Here's another. This one is the last I'll name. He

was secretary to the First Continental Congress and carried the news to George Washington of his election to the presidency. He translated the Pentateuch from the Greek. In his old age he destroyed all his personal papers to avoid passing on to his innocent countrymen a true version of the trashy quarrels of the Founding Fathers. He never lived in the wild Mississippi Territory, but his collateral descendants did. I do not know whether he owned slaves.

The plan for an uprising, purportedly made shortly after the beginning of the Civil War by certain slaves in Adams County, if it existed, was not implemented. The names of some of the owners of some of the slaves implicated and of men involved in the "Examination" and eventual execution of at least thirty of these slaves were Dunbar, Henderson, Surget, Conner, Minor, Shields—and others.

One of my grandmothers was married to the son and grandson of Surgets and Dunbars. The other was born a Henderson. Both were born in 1860 and lived into their nineties. Both were dedicated storytellers. I knew, because they told me, what it was like to live in Adams County in the last third of the nineteenth century. I knew that spiderwebs were used on bleeding wounds to induce clotting. I knew that family prayers were held every night and that children memorized their Catechism: *What is sin? Sin is any want of conformity unto or transgression of the law of God.* I knew that young ladies were never left alone with young men, not even their fiancés. I knew that the dining room table I ate at every time I visited my maternal grandmother had been fished out of the river after a paddle wheeler exploded and sank north of Natchez. I knew, because she told me, that the mistresses of plantations were called into service by tenants whose wives were enduring hard births. I knew that she (Grandmother One) had delivered a dead baby after a two-day-long labor by one of these women, and also that she had induced labor in herself during an unwanted pregnancy and had aborted early, stillborn, what seemed to be twin fetuses. I knew that long ago there had been a man in the remote northern part of the county whose daughters (after the death of their mother) were used by their father in a game called fox-hunt, the conclusion of which was the capture of the girls and their sexual use by the father's hunting companions. (My grandmother said the hunters were black men, but this seemed implausible to me.) In any case, when this horror was revealed, the father was waited on by the "gentlemen of the neighborhood" and given twenty-four hours to leave the county. The secret of what had happened to the girls was kept by the whole community, my grandmother said. They were sent away to convent school and later made suitable marriages in another part of the country.

But I never knew until a couple of years ago that the Plan existed (or was fabricated) or that the torture and executions of thirty or more slaves took place at the race-track and near The Forest Church, perhaps on Brighton Woods Plantation, or on Cherry Grove.

Dunbar, Henderson, Surget, Conner, Shields, Minor. Like Charlemagne, the bearers of these names had descendants who persisted in continuing to marry one another. I am descended from or "connected with" all of them.

But you can see how little such connections resemble our continent-wide connection with Charlemagne. Can anyone imagine claiming the nearsighted gene as an inheritance from him, or worrying about how many Saxons he killed? But these people on the wall, I know their faces, arrogant or solemn or timid or gently smiling, their wire-rimmed glasses, their hidden red coats, as well as I know the face of the gentle, retiring, rigidly private aunt for whom I am named, the aunt, dead just ten years, whose photograph is on my desk, who would not forgive my violation on this page of her privacy. It's as if, like my aunt, the people on the wall seem to have dropped only temporarily from our lives. I might find that, after all, they've just gone to Memphis to visit cousins. Or like my aunt they're in heaven. If I get there, not only will I recognize them, but they will recognize me. We know each other. We are responsible to each other. We hold each other accountable.

1975: Moving Continental Plates

A number of years ago I learned, by accident, as it seemed at the time, of the long-past suicide of my grandfather. I was present at a family gathering of the four of us siblings at our yearly board of directors meeting, as we called it, for we jointly own a tree farm in Adams County, on Second Creek, and each year we have to decide what trees to cut and what to do with the modest income. The farm is the site of my father's boyhood home, a house built (or bought—we're not sure which) by his great-grandfather around 1800.

It's dusk on a spring afternoon and, as always at these gatherings, we're having drinks on the long front gallery, looking out with pleasure across the shadowy lawn with its ancient cedar and live oak trees, and catching up on family news. For some reason—I've entirely forgotten how it came up—my older sister and I are talking about old times, family history, perhaps about our grandmother's courage in the lean years following her husband's death, perhaps about how her brother-in-law helped keep the wolf from her door until the children were all grown and launched into the world.

"Didn't they move in with Great-Grandmother Chamberlain? I think they did—after he killed himself." This from my older sister, Anna.

"Who killed himself?" I say.

"That's when they moved in with great-grandmother," my sister said again. "When Grandfather killed himself."

"What do you mean?" I said. "Grandfather died of apoplexy."

"No," Anna said. "He killed himself."

Ice tinkled in her highball glass as she took a sip. The wind stirred her graying hair, stirred the moss in the cedar trees, whoosh, lifted the scattered leaves under the live oaks, and subsided.

"Archer," I said to my younger sister, "did Grandfather Davis commit suicide?"

"Hmm?" Archer said. She was not much interested in this ancient history. Then, "Mama said he died of apoplexy. Out on that farm he was renting. Up near—where? On the way to Fayette?"

"On Tacony," I said. "Over the river. In Louisiana."

"Father told me he killed himself," Anna said stubbornly. *"Father told me."*

"You're imagining things. You must have dreamed it."

"He had a stroke," Archer said. "Where did you get the idea that he killed himself?"

All three of us sisters are graying now. We're slender and we still carry ourselves with shoulders back, as our mother taught us. Otherwise we're very different from one another, I think. Anna is the leader, head of the family; Archer is devout. And I? I'm writing this.

Anna was sitting in the brown wicker rocker that had once been our grandmother's. She rocked back now, and then forward, set her glass on the table beside her, gave me an ironic big-sisterly look. "You put his death on Tacony in your first book," she said to me. "They'd lost Tacony several years before he died. Archer's right. He was farming up north of town somewhere."

My head had begun to ache. "He had a stroke," I said again. "Everybody knew that."

"Sometimes you confuse what really happened with what you make up for your books," Anna said. "I always assumed you had him die of apoplexy in the book because it was a secret. The suicide, I mean."

"In the book! In the book! Grandfather isn't in the book. The book is fiction. Made up."

"Sure," Anna said. "Of course." She picked up her glass, smiled at me over the rim.

I kept shaking my head. "Why didn't Father tell *us?* Archer and me? Why did he just tell you?"

At this point our brother, Dick, came out on the gallery, gin and tonic in hand, and looked at us curiously. Clearly something was up.

"Tell me I'm not crazy, Dick," Anna said. "Tell me how Grandfather Davis died."

Dick shook his head. He was reluctant to speak of that old, tangled, grievous time. "Can I fix anybody a drink?" he said.

"They don't believe me," Anna said.

He's very erect, almost swaybacked, my brother (as my father was), and he carries himself as my father did, like a soldier. Now he shifted his shoulders inside his loose sport shirt as if they might be cramping. Then he said, "He shot himself. He committed suicide."

"Mama knew," Anna said, "and Charles [her younger brother], but not the rest of them—I think."

Two crows flew up with raucous cries from the tallest cedar tree in the middle of the front yard.

We sat looking at each other. For me it was as if the continental plate of our family life had moved ever so slightly, as if a crack were widening in the yard in front of the house, an earthquake beginning. The ancient, twisted *Magnolia fuscata* by the steps (killed to the ground in the freeze of '95, our father used to say) heaved and shook. A section of the 150-year-old picket fence wavered and righted itself. The live oak tree quaked.

"There are lots of things about it I don't know," Anna said. "But this is what Father told me."

My grandfather died in "the prime of life." I had from childhood a vivid mental image of him riding his spirited horse through a field of shoulder-high cotton (cotton used to be taller) on a hot September day, his face flushed with the heat, bolls popping open all around him. Then, he's dead. He's lying in the field. The horse has galloped riderless to the barn. My grandfather has left behind him a widow, a twenty-two-year-old married son, three daughters—eighteen, twelve, and nine—a son, seven, and a bankrupt estate. County records of the probate of his will indicate that when the debts were paid the sum of six hundred dollars was left for his widow and minor children.

When I was a child there was no portrait of my grandfather on anyone's wall. Of course, by the time he was a grown man, toward the end of Reconstruction, few people in the South had money to pay for portraits. But my grandmother had a photograph of him on her bedroom mantel. He is a handsome, vigorous man in his late forties, with dark, curly hair and swarthy skin, evidence perhaps of Creole genes—one of his grand-mothers was a Surget and one a Vidal. A heavy mustache conceals his lips.

"Oh, he was a charmer," my grandmother would say when I asked about him. But then she'd add, "A reader, too, studious."

My mother told me that when there was not enough money to afford a tutor and the nearest school was miles away over the river in Natchez, he assigned his children reading from his library—Dickens, Thack-eray, Scott, Cooper, Bulwer-Lytton, Macaulay, Gibbon —and required of them written reports.

"He never bothered with spelling or arithmetic," my mother said. "You see the result in me."

He kept game cocks. He was a fine shot. And courageous, too, my grandmother would add—fighting flood and boll weevil and bankruptcy.

Oh, the tragedy of it, to die so young, so vital, to leave fatherless children, a grieving widow.

"Jo [her sister] was his darling," my mother said, "and she adored him. I don't think she ever got over his death. I remember him as sterner, more demanding."

All this as I was growing up. Later the first cracks began to appear, although I didn't recognize them as cracks until later, counted them instead a result of the natural jealousy of a first daughter replaced by a new baby, jealousy masked by finding fault with the unfaithful father.

My mother spoke of how after his death they had lived on the edge of poverty. Her older brother, Vidal, already married and with a baby, had his own responsibilities. She, at eighteen, went to work at whatever she could turn her hand to. She taught for a while, had a dance studio, acted as companion to a dull and crotchety rich lady. Her mother rented rooms to respectable gentlemen, turned a part of the house into a rental apartment. Her father's faraway, wealthy brother-in-law sent the family a regular small check. These, of course, were all reasonable remedies in their predicament. But this is the first crack: "Those years before he died," she once said to me, "after we moved back to town, when he was riding the ferry over the river every day to Tacony, he'd run up a bar bill in the ferry bar. Ninety or a hundred dollars every month. And we were already in trouble—it was after that second bad flood. Nineteen eight, 1909?"

"Mama! A hundred dollars? That would be like five hundred dollars now. A thousand."

"It wasn't that he drank too much," she said. "He wasn't an alcoholic. But he would always buy a round or two for everybody in the bar. He was open handed. He loved a party."

"But Mama! . . ."

"Yes," she said. "It's hard for me to forgive him that. I don't think the girls [her younger sisters] ever knew about it. But I did."

Stern and demanding to one, an adoring father to the other. Resourceful and studious. Recklessly open handed and party loving. Well, people are full of contradictions, aren't they?

I remember, too, now I think about it, that she told me once how he had suffered as a child from the severity of his stepmother, who was partial to her own children.

I did not notice that my mother had no photograph of her father in our house. Of us, her children, of our father, of her mother and her sisters, but not of him. The only photographs of him I ever saw belonged to my grandmother and my two aunts.

So this new lesson in family history, learned late in life, long after I thought I understood us all pretty well, was about vanishing people. The charming, open-handed Creole gentleman, the adoring father with the jealous older daughter, the husband whose photograph I'd seen from childhood on my grandmother's mantelpiece, vanished one day when I was a woman in my fifties, sitting happily on the gallery visiting with my siblings and drinking a bourbon old-fashioned, vanished

behind the heavy shadow of suicide and, worse, abandonment of his young family to hardship and poverty.
The Creole gent got on his fine, spirited horse and rode
away and I never saw him again.

I hear Gold Sr. now interrupting this story, as
he did an earlier one. "But wait a minute," he's saying.
He's laughing at me. "You wrote down something else,
didn't you?" he says. "In some book or other. In your
book, that other book, you turned your grandpa into a
great-great-aunt. You told a whole nother story about
her and her suicide—made it OK for her to kill herself.
How come you to do that?"

"*You* know," I say. "You of all people know how
come me to do that."

"Hmmm," he says. "'Twas for your convenience I
reckon."

"I reckon," I said. "For the convenience of the story.
For the story."

*A*nother thing is true, I notice here: I have no
compunction about writing this new version of my
grandfather's death, concealed so long, and at what cost
to my mother I will never know. She is dead. They are
all dead, his sons and daughters, taking their secrets, their
illusions, their pain and grief and lies and loves to the

grave with them. And we survivors are left to parse things out for ourselves, to clutch our own secrets to our breasts, baffle our grandchildren.

Besides, as I found out later, there is this curious fact. In a way, his suicide has long been a matter of public record. In the church register, beside his name and the date of his death, someone has written in a different hand and with different-colored ink, the word "Suicide." Who wrote it? When? For what reason? We will never know, but there it is for anyone to see, and that in itself would make a story.

From her early thirties on, my mother lived in a world muffled by increasing deafness. She lived to be eighty-seven years old. I was fifty-seven when she died. I could not have written this while she was alive: Her death freed me from the obligation to cause her no more pain than I had to. She died believing that she took with her the knowledge that her father had chosen to kill himself rather than stay and struggle to protect the lives of his young family. For more than sixty years she must have shielded her mother and her sisters from this knowledge. She had had to listen to their voices, distorted by her hearing aid, recounting again and again to her children the romance of his life—his Creole good looks, his élan, his game cocks, his charming friends, his courage, his resilience. No wonder she was deaf.

My father told my sister Anna and my younger brother, when they were grown, of their grandfather's suicide, and enjoined them not to speak of this old tragedy to anyone, especially not to my mother, my grandmother, and my aunts. Our mother knew, he said, but she never spoke about it, even to him. He had always known, he said, but she had found out, after she was grown and married, by accident, in a way. "It was your uncle Charles," he said. "Accidents are always happening with Charles."

This is what happened, my father said.

Mr. Davis was farming on a place a few miles north of Natchez on the Mississippi side of the river. He had already lost Tacony, the family farm on the Louisiana side. He would catch a northbound train every morning, ride out to where he'd left his horse stabled, and from there ride out to the farm. He boarded the train that morning as usual, saw a friend and chatted with him cheerfully, got off the train as usual, got his horse, rode out to the farm, and shot himself. At this point, someone must have gotten word to his son Vidal in Natchez and somehow, for some reason, the deception began.

Years later, after my parents were married, after Anna and I were born, my mother's younger brother, Charles, came visiting one winter. This would have been not long after the First World War and her brother would have been still in his twenties. He got drunk, my father told Anna, and disabused my mother of the fairy tale of her father's apoplexy: September heat, ripening cotton, spirited horse and spirited man.

She never forgave him for telling her, my father said, and she must have put the fear of God in him, for apparently he never got drunk enough to tell his mother and his other sisters. *She never forgave him for telling her.* I find that exceedingly curious. Why was his telling her unforgivable? Was it that she could not bear being told a truth every hint of which, at enormous cost to herself, she had closed away and forgotten or had refused to recognize? Or was it, perhaps, my father who never forgave him? And how did my father know? Did everyone in that small world know, except the dead man's wife and daughters? I am as baffled as I was at Gold's account of the white man who would "help the people with their papers." Something is missing.

It is impossible to make sense out of stories that purport to be true. Something is always missing. To give them form, extract their deepest meaning, one has to turn them into fiction, to find causes, or if, as is usually the case, causes are unfindable, one has to invent them.

It's said that the tremor of a butterfly's wing in Sumatra could be the triggering event that sends a hurricane to drive a tanker over the sea wall into the front yard of a home in Gulfport, Mississippi. But surely the causes of human tragedy, arising from human passion, are not so tenuous, so easily overlooked.

All these silences, all these unfinished tales, these lacunae in the evidence, are intolerable to me. *What kind of people are these?* I keep asking myself. No. Not *What kind of people are these,* but *What kind are* we?

Do you understand what I am saying here?

1. My father knew before he married her that his wife's father committed suicide. He knew that she did not know it and he did not reveal his knowledge to her.
2. Her older brother and her younger brother knew, but not her sisters or her mother.
3. A doctor must surely have signed the death certificate. He must either have falsified the cause of death or called in the sheriff. If the latter, the sheriff must have colluded with him in concealing the cause of death. (This is clearly ridiculous. What possible reason would he have for doing such a thing?)

Questions: Who found the body? Who carried the news down to Natchez? What was the undertaker's role? What was my uncle Vidal's role? Was there a suicide note? Did my grandmother know or suspect the truth and keep silent? Why, why, why not grieve openly for this loss, this act of rejection? Why not weep and scream together and comfort one another and lay him to rest? Is this silence extraordinarily relevant to the time and place these lives were lived out? Or to something else?

And finally, there is this, which I have thought of only in recent years, only since I began to put down this record: Did he commit suicide at all? Is it possible that all this elaborate concealment conceals not a suicide but a murder? Did someone whom it was necessary to protect murder him? Or did the murderer fake the suicide? Was it the case that even his son Vidal did not know what really happened? That my mother's terrible silent grief, my scorn at his abandonment of his family, are wrong, all wrong? Perhaps she, too, thought of this possibility and wondered and wondered at the reasons for her older brother's silence. Ah, there's a whole novel to dream over.

None of these questions will ever be answered: Together we have buried the answers.

Later: One question is, after all, answerable, as I learned from the records of the funeral parlor that received his body. The doctor who signed the death certificate, entering the cause of death as suicide, was Charles Chamberlain, my grandmother's nephew, my mother's first cousin. But this fact makes all that happened even more deeply mysterious. The men in the family and the community must have closed ranks. But why?

My father and his father and his father's mother grew up in the house where we sat on the gallery that spring afternoon and drank our old-fashioneds and watched the crows fly up from the shivering cedar trees.

Years ago, in the 1920s, when my father's maiden aunt was dying, she instructed my father and his brothers to bring a particular trunk full of letters and diaries —letters that went back to the early 1800s—down from the attic of that house and burn them.

"I never could persuade myself to do it," she said.

Letters between her grandfather and his wife and children and the families they had left back in Maryland, and his sister and her family who had settled in Louisiana.

"I never could persuade myself," she said. "You'll have to do it."

"Father!" I said when he told me this. "Did you?"

He nodded. "She asked us to. We promised."

"Did you read them?" I said.

"No," he said. "She didn't give us permission to read them."

My mother told me once that when she married

my father she knew that his maiden aunt (the lady who told her nephews to destroy the family papers) opposed the marriage. Later, though, as my mother slowly coaxed the old lady out of her shyness, and particularly after she named her first child Anna for this aunt, they became friends, such good friends that one day, as they were sitting together "visiting," she summoned the courage to ask what it was the aunt had had against her. My mother knew that she was a young lady of good family, attractive, intelligent, devout enough—a Presbyterian, even —to have been deemed a suitable mate for my father, and so Aunt Anna's opposition puzzled her.

In my imagination I see them now, as I would dramatize this scene. My great-aunt's face floods with color, then pales. She shakes her head, covers her mouth with that characteristic family gesture of shyness, denial. *I will not speak.*

"Never mind," my mother says. "You needn't tell me if you don't want to."

My great-aunt is silent for a few moments. She bends over, makes a pretext of rolling a ball toward her namesake, who is sitting on the floor between them. Then, "Oh, it's ridiculous, Laura, too ridiculous." She clasps her hands in her lap, leans forward. She's smiling, ready to tell a funny story of which she's the butt. "I was worried about whether you were a serious person," she says. "I had always heard . . . I'd heard that you and Caroline Stratton . . . when you were children, of course . . . that you'd danced for pennies in the barbershop."

My mother finishes the story triumphantly. "And of course we had!" she says. "We'd wait until we knew Mr. Wheeler, Caroline's stepfather, was coming in for a shave, because he would be sure to give us each a nickel, and then . . ."

I see her as a child now, with her companion, fearless little girls, tomboys, braving the male world—the men's hogan, the sweat house of the nineteenth-century white man—to dance for pennies. Would anyone tell on them or would they get away with it—ah, there was where the thrill lay. Evidently, someone did tell Aunt Anna; but fortunately for Mother no one told my grandmother.

Having indulged myself in this fantasy, I think of something else. Perhaps Aunt Anna knows another, darker story that she does not tell, uses this one instead to satisfy my mother, keep the family facade intact.

1968: Gold Smith Jr.

Gold Jr. was a man very different from his father—and very like him. Like in the color of his skin, a smooth golden brown; like in his love of the country and his skill as a hunter, his devotion to his family; like in his high intelligence, openly evident, though, never hidden as Gold Sr.'s always was until he began to be sure that you took the same sort of pleasure in his role-playing as he did. Unlike because he was a man of a different time, faced a different world.

This is a story that Gold Sr. told my son about Gold Jr., who was a youngish married man with children during the Civil Rights struggles of the 1960s and 1970s.

Again I hear Gold Sr.'s voice, see his skeptical face, his secretive smile. "Wait a minute here," he says to me. "You done it again, didn't you? Took what happen to Gold and put it in a book and put a made-up name to it. Gold never had no affair with a white woman, a divorced woman out looking for danger, for a thrill. I shouldn't have told that story about him and the supervisor for you to use like you did."

"Come on," I say. "What about *The floors was made of plush?* What about *hair like ropes of gold, thick enough to keep her warm?* What about *ladles full of money?* The love affair in my book, Sam and Leila's affair, that was for the story. What I want to do now is to give Gold's part of that story back to him, back to the man it belongs to."

During the years of the Civil Rights struggle, Gold Smith Jr. worked at the Armstrong Rubber Company in Natchez. He was one of the men who agitated for equal jobs and equal pay in the union there—a union always heretofore controlled by and for the benefit of its white members, many of whom belonged to the Klan. Here, as elsewhere in the country, the struggle for racial equality in the union—equal jobs, equal pay, equal seniority—was a bitter battle. There were car bombings. Men were murdered. Gold, whom every friend I've talked with characterized as a persistent man, persisted. He had accidents that seemed to him and them not to be accidents. But he persisted. It happened one day that he walked up the long, steep driveway of his country house to his mailbox to pick up his mail and found painted on the blacktop road in broad stripes of white, a cross, perhaps eight feet long and four feet wide—big enough so that he couldn't miss it. He went back into the house and telephoned his supervisor, the elected official who was in charge of roads and streets and garbage collection in the district—an elderly white man known to be no more and no less racist than most elderly white men in the neighborhood.

"I got something to show you," Gold said, "something you need to see."

The supervisor came by in his pickup truck with the CB radio antenna and the gun rack across the back and together they examined the cross.

"What do you think of that?" Gold said.

"Well, Gold," the old man said, "looks like they put their mark on you, don't it?"

"Ain't it fortunate I'm such a good shot," Gold said. "You know—you and me have hunted together. Ain't it fortunate?"

"You right about one thing," the supervisor said. "You're a good shot."

Whether or not his markmanship had anything to do with it, Gold survived those years, survived persistent journeying about the state organizing blacks in other plants, driving from meeting to meeting at night, far from home, alone because there was no one brave enough to go with him, survived months-long boycotts, survived all-night vigils in the homes of threatened activists, survived protest marches for school integration, survived "accidents" of various sorts—as did many of his peers all over the country. It was a time the heroisms of which are mostly forgotten. And now I want to give his heroism, which I used to create a character in a novel to whom I gave another life and other problems, back to him and his family.

As to why this act has come to seem more and more

important to me, this has to do with the slave uprising on Second Creek in 1861.

1861: Obey, a Slave, and Others

The envelope in the LSU archives containing Lemuel Conner's account of the "proceedings" had written on it the following:

> "there were <u>ten</u> slaves hung in Brighton Woods and Cherry Grove
> Documents about Uprising of <u>Slaves</u> about 1860–61
> Your <u>Grandfather L. P. Conner's</u> (Senior) own handwriting <u>the testimony</u> of negro slaves.

A covering note in the same hand reads:

> Please <u>take very special care</u> of these four sheets of paper! <u>They are exceeding</u> interesting, exceedingly important as they are the <u>literal, original, testimony taken down</u> by Lemuel Parker Conner at the time of the <u>trial</u> of some Adams County negro slaves. Tis put down just as these negro men expressed it. This L. P. C. <u>Senior</u> was the father of L. P. C. Jr. (your Dad—I wish this <u>Kept</u>—together with envelopes, papers and all.

This is the document that lay for years in the cabinet beside the bed of Lemuel and Mary Conner, Liza Conner Martin's parents. The note on the outside of the envelope must have been written by Mary. It was Mary, then, the lady who made paths of broken glass and china for the fairies and told the children stories, Mary, the actress who was not considered a serious person—it was she and not Lemuel Conner Jr. who adjured their children to preserve this record.

Here are the names of some of the owners and some of their slaves who were examined during the proceedings at The Forest (the Dunbar place, on the south end of Second Creek) and at the racetrack on St. Catherine Creek, a couple of miles from downtown Natchez, on Cherry Grove and Brighton Woods:

Ike Giddings and Adam Giddings, owned by A. C. Henderson of Grove Plantation. Mr. Henderson's grandmother had been a Giddings. Perhaps these slaves came from her estate. His grandfather was the Dickens clerk who wrote *Paine Detected*, whose portrait hangs now on my dining room wall.

Billy and Obey, owned by Jacob Surget of Cherry Grove Plantation. Mr. Surget, who, some sources say, owned ten thousand slaves, was not in Mississippi at the time of the "trial."

Lee Scott, owned by Katherine Minor, whose husband, John Minor, was present at some of the proceedings and who later sued the federal government for the return of her property on the basis of her husband's record as a federal sympathizer.

Dick and Peter, father and son, both literate, and George, brother to Dick, all owned by Mrs. Mary Dunbar, widow of William Dunbar Jr. of The Forest.

Harry Lyle, owned by a man named Mitchell, owner of Palatine Plantation.

Not examined was a slave named Orange belonging to a man named Mosby, on whose plantation John Austin and his son Benny lived—Benny who may have been the person who reported the Plan to his white family. Orange was gone. Orange had run away.

No one kept a record of what happened at the racetrack, where twenty more slaves were killed; but we know the name of the leader of this group, Bill Postlethwaite. We do not know what happened to him.

The Conner account contains the names of a number of other slaves and owners as well as other participants in the examinations, but my purpose here is not to follow Winthrop Jordan's argument regarding the events of the nonuprising. I wish to write about other matters.

For a long time I thought about, looked for ways into a novel in which Benny would be the center of the narrative—the mysterious Benny who must have told some other white person of the slaves' conversation about killing the masters and "riding" the ladies (or in some cases, as Conner's record shows, "taking them as wives") when Mr. Lincoln and the Yankees came. Jordan deduces from fragile census information that Benny was probably the nine-year-old son of John Austin, manager on the Mosby plantation, where Orange and his son Harvey were slaves. Harvey may have been one of the slaves who was killed. Benny is never identified in the testimony of the slaves as anyone other than "Mas' Benny" who "asked why"—why "the whipping would stop" after Lincoln came. The only references to him in Conner's record are from two slaves who say he *asked why.*

There is no way, unless some other archival information comes to light, to know certainly who Benny was. The novelist would have a free hand. What I was meditating on was what might happen in the life of a man who knew that he had, as a child, by reporting what he heard, caused the torture and death of so many companions and guardians—beloved companions, as black men often were in those days to the male children of their white masters.

Even more terrible, is it possible that *nothing happened*—nothing was ever muttered by anyone, that Benny, whoever he was, whatever his motives, made up the tale of hearing the slaves talk of an uprising? What could I do with this supposition?

Later, as an alternative way into this material, I thought about the slaves who were silent under examination, whose lives and voices are lost forever. What kind of men were these? Could I imagine their lives?

In Conner's notes, each slave's testimony about the "conspiracy," "The Plan," as it is called in Jordan's book, is given beneath his name. There is no way for the reader to know what the questions are, who asks them, or what happens between answers. Here is the last part of the record, after a number of the slaves have been examined, some twice, and have spoken at length, naming names, making accusations, incriminating themselves. In the case of five slaves—John, Obey, Billy, Adam, and Harry Lyle—there are the following entries:

> Mitchells boy <u>Harry Lyle</u> says OO—
> Hendersons boy <u>Adam</u> says Orange told him what amts to nothing—
> <u>John</u> (Little) belongs to J N Mitchell says Orange told him on the Creek, that—OO—
> Capt Surgets boy <u>Obey</u>—says nothing—
> Capt Surgets boy <u>Billy</u> says nothing.

Several more slaves are then examined and are more forthcoming. Harvey, for example, says: "I talked to

Obey next to Mr Metcalfe's. Says I, [']Obey, our folks join the Northerners.['] Obey said I will join them too to help kill the white folks."

Here is the end of the manuscript. Obey has obviously been brought back:

Obey, Obey, Obey, John O. Fenall, Obey, Obey, Obey, Obey, Obey, Obey, Obey, Obey.
end

Harry Scott

"I will kill old master and ride the ladies." Orange says Mrs Griffith's black man said most time for work. Dick read dispatch. George too. Dick was religious man. Dick and George and Peter can read. Simon has a gun—George too.

<u>George</u>

" " " " " " " " " " " " " "

Alfred

<u>Dick</u>

Here the manuscript ends. The reader is left to guess who John O. Fenall was (he is mentioned nowhere else), what questions were asked, what threats made, what other measures taken, what "end" after the string of "Obey's" means, what happened to George and Alfred and Dick—to any of these men.

Evidence of coercion comes from other manuscript

sources. First, there is an extant letter found by Winthrop Jordan in the course of his research. It is from a white eyewitness to a part of the proceedings of the committee and is dated October 25, 1861: "<u>Eight Negroes swung off one plank and hung, and two whipped to death dying under the lash.</u> Twenty others were hung two weeks or so ago. . . . All testimony was extracted from the negroes by whipping—."

Second, there is the testimony of an ex-slave, James Carter, in a federal property suit brought by Mrs. Katherine Minor thirteen years after the war. This suit is a claim against the federal government for reimbursement of moneys lost as a result of federal action during the war. Mrs. Minor sues as a Union sympathizer. Her husband's presence at the proceedings of the committee (which would, of course, have undermined her claim) is being argued. Mrs. Minor claims that his presence was for the purpose of moderating the proceedings. James Carter, however, says that "Mr. Minor questioned me as much as any of them." Here is his account of the questioning:

> The final day they carried me out then they whipped me terribly. Several of them were whipping me at once . . . The object . . . was to make me confess . . . I told them I knew nothing about it, which was the truth. They said they would make me know, and

then they whipped me. They would whip until I fainted and then stop and whip again. Dr Harper sat by and would feel my pulse and tell them when to stop and when to go on. . . . [E]ight of the men were hung in my presence. There were eighteen of us, eight were hung and ten of were left. They then said to me that they had concluded not to hang me but would give me a whipping and send me home.

Mrs. Minor, of course, had her own witnesses, black and white. The federal government awarded her $13,000 of her $58,000 claim.

Whether or not the conversations about Mr. Lincoln and the Yankees took place, the men were hanged or beaten to death. Did Benny perhaps fabricate what he reported out of whole cloth or on the basis of half-heard or misunderstood mutterings? Did the men being tortured admit to anything, anything at all, that would stop the beatings, knowing that no matter what they said, they would die? In any case, they died—the ten at Forest Church and the twenty at the racetrack.

When I read Winthop Jordan's book, when I saw the names of Alexander Henderson (my great-great-uncle); of Mary Dunbar, daughter-in-law of the gentleman who painted his red coat black; of Captain Jacob Surget, great-uncle of my suicidal grandfather; and others, too—Conner, Shields, Minor, Martin, all "connections"—my first overwhelming impulse was to say to myself: *How could this be?* Not only how could it have happened, but how could such a huge event in the history of a small county not be known to me? To all of us. To the world.

And later, finally, thinking about stories, about novels, I dreamed this story:

Orange. What about Orange, who ran away? Orange, who, his friends reported, had said, "We will be done with whipping before long." What about Bill Postlethwaite, who was probably the leader of the Natchez group?

In my story Orange and Bill Postlethwaite escape.

They are befriended by a rawboned white man, not tall, "looked like an Irishman" (Nelson, another Mosby slave, described this man), or by someone else—a white man who painted his face black or a man with red hair and small feet, a German, a Dutchman who wore a wool hat, a barefoot white man, or a woman, Mrs. King, who is a fortune-teller, tells fortunes with cards. These are all people, accomplices (imaginary people?) mentioned during the examinations by one or another of the slaves who talked.

In my story Orange and Bill hide with Mrs. King (a gypsy?) and then, before they can be apprehended and examined, melt into the deep woods. They make their way northward, enduring great hardships: swarming mosquitoes and horseflies, bloodsucking ticks, thickets of briers, impenetrable canebrakes, swamps through which they wade, thigh-deep in mud. By day they hide in the canebrakes, cover their bodies with mud to escape the swarming insects. Below Vicksburg they find an abandoned pirogue and under cover of darkness paddle across the Mississippi River. Deep in a canebrake, a part of the Louisiana Delta still untouched by the death-dealing hand of the white man, they connect with a wandering band of Caddo Indians. Or perhaps their benefactors are redbones, those mysterious Louisianians purported to be descendants of members of Laffite's pirate band who bred with Indians and escaped slaves. In any case, they are taken in and fed and sheltered and hidden. They are brave and patient and intelligent men and they survive the war years. They change their names.

Bill Postlethwaite marries a half-Indian woman who is the legal owner of a small piece of land in Tensas Parish. Like many black people early and late, their children lose the land to the owner of a very large nearby plantation. Hampton, my grandmother's chauffeur, is the grandson of one of their children. (His mother, as he had once told me, "had Indian blood.")

Orange, after the war, makes his way back to Natchez and rejoins his family, learns at last of the death of his son, Harvey. Walking down St. Catherine Street in Natchez one day, he sees a young white man, a boy of seventeen or eighteen, on a roan mare. Horse and man look familiar to him, although the man was a child when last he saw him. *That's Mas' Benny,* he says to himself.

"Hey, Benny," someone calls to the rider. And the young man pulls up his horse and stops.

That's Benny Austin. Yes it is. Benny, who blew the whistle on us, and Bill and me were the only ones that got away.

I think Orange devoted himself to observing Benny's habits. I think he bided his time and made his plans and one night when Benny was riding home alone on the Woodville Road, his horse shied at something, no one ever knew what, and threw Benny, and Benny broke his neck and died there in the road. Before he died he saw Orange bending over him, looking down at him. He looked into Orange's eyes and knew him.

Not long afterwards Orange and his family set out northward. They were not waylaid by Paterollers or jailed as vagrants and impressed into chain gangs. They did not starve to death. (Orange had acquired valuable skills in his years with the Caddo or the redbones.) They may have settled in New England. Their descendants are graduates of Harvard and other fine schools.

This is the story I want to tell. I want a happy ending—for *someone.* But I have only the story that is told in Lemuel Conner's notes.

1922: Hope, Arkansas

Years ago, my mother told me of driving for the first time with my father and older sister into the little town of Hope, Arkansas, where all of us would live happily for some years. Coming into town, she said, they saw, as you always see first in little towns, the standpipe, the water tower, looming over the town's highest building, in this case, a three-story hotel. She saw, hanging from the metal struts, the body of a black man. He had been lynched and left hanging, a warning to uppity niggers. She said nothing to my father, was intent rather on keeping my sister from seeing this terrible sight. But that night, when Anna was safely asleep, she wept. "We can't live here, Richardson," she said to my father. "Take us away. Take us back to civilization. Take us back to Natchez where things like this don't happen."

Surely, to be able to speak as she did, my honorable mother could not have known of the proceedings of the committee of gentlemen of the neighborhood, the executions at the racetrack, the beatings and hangings at Forest Church.

Like my mother, I had never heard one hint, one breath, one word regarding these matters. To all of us, lynching was unspeakable. And our ancestors, the portraits on the walls—they had been kind masters who treated their slaves with consistent humanity.

Let me say here parenthetically that, so far as could be ascertained by Jordan, although the slaves were theirs, no Henderson, Dunbar, or Surget was present at the proceedings of the committee, either at the racetrack or at Forest Church (or Brighton Woods or Cherry Grove). William Dunbar Jr. was dead. Jacob Surget was in New York. As for where Alexander Henderson was, it remains a mystery. Who represented these owners? Who spoke for them? And what did their representatives say? Did they stand by and see these slaves killed? Did they consent? Did they assist? Again, we shall never know. The long silence had begun.

And was it shame that prevented anyone from talking of such terrible matters? Yes. Shame and fear. Fear had made it happen and shame had enforced the silence. It was late 1861, remember, in a world where there were ten slaves to every white person. The white men were mostly gone—off at war. There was fear at the heart of every slave owner's household. And afterwards, the silence was never broken.

But these explanations are not good enough, are they? Perhaps they're not even true. There is the possibility, for example, that they feared knowledge of these matters, of their summary—but correct—dealing with these criminals, would fire the zeal of abolitionists and strengthen the Yankee cause.

1776: *Richmond, Louisiana*

*H*ere are three entries from the first William Dunbar's day book, kept at his plantation at Richmond, Louisiana, from 1776 until 1780, published in 1930, along with other papers and letters, by the Mississippi Historical Society. I have owned a copy of this book for many years. The first entry concerns an aborted plot among the slaves on Dunbar's Louisiana plantation at Richmond in 1776.

> They [The gentlemen of the neighborhood] informed me that a conspiracy among . . . Negroes had been discovered, & that it had taken [plac]e at my House. The Names of three were mentioned, who with a Negro of Watt's & Flowers, were said to be the principals—Judge my surprise! Of what avail is kindness & good usage when rewarded by such in-

gratitude; 'tis true indeed they were kept under due
subordination & obliged to do their duty in respect
to plantation work, but two of the three had always
behaved so well that they had never once received a
stroke of the whip—I immediately sent to the field
where they were a making staves to call in one of
the Principalls, whom I carried up with me to Mr.
Poupets in company with Francis & Gordon . . .
When questioned he seemed to know nothing of
the matter, & when confronted by Mr. Ross' Negroes / the Informers / who had the story from himself, he still persisted in his Inocence & Ignorance &
mentioned as an argument why it must be impossible; that he had now b[een] Considerable time with
his Master, that he had fed & clothed him well &
had never once struck him & of course it was absurd
to suppose him guilty. In the afternoon we set out
on our return down with Mr. Poupet to seize the
rest of the criminals—My Negro was sitting in the
bottom of the Boat with his arms pinioned; He was
'tis supposed stung with the heghnousness of his
guilt, ashamed perhaps to look a Master in the face
against whom he could urge no plea to paliate his
intended Diabolical plan; for he took an oppy. in
the middle of the River to throw himself overboard
& was immediately drowned—This was sufficient
evidence of his guilt . . . The Monday following
was appointed for the trial of the Criminals & no-

tice was sent to the neighbouring settlements to be
present on so solemn an occasion . . . When our
two Negroes and one of Watt's & Flower were condemned to be hanged & were accordingly executed
. . . Lesser punishments were inflicted on the less
guilty . . .

The second entry, a couple of weeks later, concerns
a female slave who had run away and been recaptured:
"ordered the Wench Bessy out of Irons, & to receive 25
lashes with a Cow Skin as a punishment & Example to
the rest."

The third entry:

on sunday, eight days, Two negroes ran away but
were catched & brought back, wednesday after.
Condemned them to receive 500 lashes Each at 5
Dift. times, & to carry a chain & log fixt to the
ancle — Poor Ignorant Devils; for what do they run
away? They are well cloathed, work easy, and have
all kinds of Plantation produce at no allowance —
After a slighter Chastisement than was intended they
were set again at liberty & behave well —

There is only one other entry in Dunbar's daybook
regarding punishments. A slave, Adam, found drunk
on rum, is threatened with "500 lashes" if he doesn't
disclose the source of the rum. This "had the desired

effect" and Dunbar wrote, "I intend carrying him up to Point Coupee, where I shall sell him if I find an opportunity . . ."

I have dipped into Dunbar's papers and letters occasionally over the years, interested in his correspondence with Thomas Jefferson, his survey for the Spanish of the boundaries of West Florida, and his account of the expedition he headed to explore the reaches of the Red and Arkansas Rivers. He wrote, too, on meteorology, astronomy, and Indian sign language. I am sure that I read about "the Wench Bessy" and about the suspected insurrection that ended in the suicide of "My Negro." But it is true that I did not think about those entries when I looked at his portrait. I thought instead about family snobbery (we always called him "Sir" William, although there is no evidence he gave himself a title), and about what an interesting man he must have been. Indeed, I had forgotten about Bessy and the others until I read *Tumult and Silence at Second Creek* and began to think about the fate of Mrs. Mary Dunbar's slaves—about Dick who was literate and a religious man, and about George, his brother, who had a gun, about Peter who was also literate and a leader—and began to meditate on remembering and forgetting, on history and fiction, on the lies we live by.

My mother, like me, had read William Dunbar's papers. I don't know whether she also overlooked the references to five hundred lashes, twenty-five lashes, a slave's suicide. Was it that such happenings had never been interesting to any of us, never worth passing down, worth talking about—as it seemed to me later that Liza was uninterested in her father's role on the committee of gentlemen of the neighborhood? Slaves, after all, were possessions, not persons. They only became persons who must be protected from lynching after they were free—and of course, for some of us, not even then.

1861: Obey and Others, Again

*H*ere again are the final entries in Conner's record:

Obey, Obey, Obey, John O. Fenall, Obey, Obey, Obey, Obey, Obey Obey, Obey, Obey.
                    end

Harry Scott
"I will kill old master and ride the ladies." Orange says Mrs Griffith's black man said most time for work. Dick read dispatch. George too. Dick was re-

ligious man. Dick and George and Peter can read.
Simon has a gun—George too.

<u>George.</u>

" " " " " " " " " " " " " " " "

Alfred

<u>Dick</u>

Were George and Alfred and Dick condemned to
death by hanging? Beaten to death? Who is John O.
Fenall? And Obey, Captain Jacob Surget's Obey—is
every repetition of his name a stroke of the lash, until finally Obey dies and Conner finds himself unable to go
on? These questions can never be answered. No devices, fictional or historical, can rescue Obey and Harry
and Adam and John, Billy and George and Alfred and
Dick, from silence and oblivion.

When I was thinking, early on, that I must find out
more about all this and put down my own witness, I was
not aware that Liza Conner Martin was still alive. Other
white people—cousins and connections—I dismissed.
Anything they might have known about these events
they would have told me long ago. I was sure none of
them knew any more than I did. I should go into the
black community, I thought. The world of black
Natchez was as stable, as stay put, as the world of white
Natchez. There were more black people whose families

had lived on Second Creek for 150 years than there were white people. Surely someone, some grandmother as old as or older than I, would remember the story that her grandmother had told of an uncle, a cousin, a father who died during those terrible proceedings, or who had lived and whose scarred back she had seen—someone who would have passed that knowledge on, would have enjoined children and grandchildren and great-grandchildren to remember.

I talked to a doctor and to a lawyer, to a retired school principal, to the almost white owner of a boutique who is a descendant of Surgets, to a descendant of the free black barber of Natchez who kept a diary during the pre–Civil War years and who owned his own slaves, to retired schoolteachers and factory workers and landowners, to political activists and members of the Democratic Executive Committee, to a member of the Board of Supervisors, to the director of the museum of black history. No one remembered ever having heard of these deaths.

It seemed to me that there should be a stone set in place like the stone at Thermopylae, perhaps on The Forest Plantation or on Cherry Grove or at the site of the old racetrack. What would it read?

Go, stranger, and tell the people that we died here, under the whip, silent to the end.

1993: Gold Jr., Again

One of the last black people I talked to of these matters was Gold Smith Jr. I hoped that his father, his bardic father, or even someone of his grandfather's generation might have told him of the Plan. Perhaps his persistence, his courage, might have had their beginnings in that knowledge. I knew, too, because my son had told me, that Gold was no longer active in union or county Democratic Party affairs. He had had a stroke a year or two ago, my son said, but seemed to be recovered. I had called him earlier, asking if I might come talk with him, but at that time, although I did not know it, his brother Lawrence was dying and Gold put me off. "I'm nursing my brother," he said. "I don't have the time right now." His voice had that dead quality that comes from grief and exhaustion and I was sorry I had intruded. Later, though, some months after Lawrence's death, I tried again and we made an appointment to talk. It was a sunny fall day when I walked down the steep driveway toward his house, thinking as I walked of the day his supervisor had looked at the cross on the road and said, "Well, Gold, looks like they put their mark on you."

He was at home alone (like his mother, his wife is a teacher). He let me in and we sat a little while talking in the small, comfortable living room of his house trailer while I told him what I was looking for. But he, too, was ignorant of what had happened at the southern end of Second Creek in September and October 1861. His father had never spoken of it. By the time we talked, Gold Sr. had been dead for some years and we spoke first of him, then of Edna, and of his brother Lawrence. I did not ask why he'd lost interest in politics, was no longer the activist he had been. He was getting old himself, he was, after all, not much younger than I.

We talked instead of his growing up on a plantation in the south end of the county, about hunting, about his children, about his father and my father. After a little while he said that he had a cousin, a man in his late eighties, who lived near Sibley in the southern part of the county and that if there was anyone around who could help me, it would be him. "He lives right down there not far from the places you're talking about—Cherry Grove, The Forest—he and his family been down there for a hundred and fifty years. And he's still got his wits about him, can tell you about what it was like when he was a boy."

We set out together in my car looking for him. "He'll be home," Gold said. "He lives by himself, has family that comes and takes him where he needs to go —the store, the doctor." We were driving through a part of the county that he knew well and he pointed out the place he had grown up on, the woods where he had hunted.

But Gold's cousin had never heard of the Plan, of the "trial," of the deaths. He sent us on to a Mazique, a member of another old and widely connected black family, who sent us on to someone else. Gold relaxed a bit, seemed less remote and sorrowful, more interested in the quest. I glanced at him now and then as we drove, admiring his fine profile, the knobby, high cheek-bones, the golden skin and close-cropped hair.

It was a beautiful day. The wind blew, the trees were green and gold and bronze, cedar and pine, gum and oak and poplar. Showers of leaves gusted across the road. We had a good time together. But I learned nothing, either about the Plan or about Gold's life. I wished afterwards that I had tried to get him to speak of the days when he had been an activist, about how things had been, how he'd managed, but there was something in his demeanor that kept me quiet. Perhaps it was that the long ordeal of sitting every day with his dying brother was still too fresh in his past for me to talk of earlier ordeals. More likely it was that I expected to have years ahead in which I might talk with him about his life. But I never saw him again.

Gold had a second massive stroke and died in late December of that same year, 1993. I was in Natchez at the time, still on my fruitless quest, and I went to his funeral. I have been to many funerals in my life, most of white friends and relatives, but some of black. This one was unlike any I had attended.

1996: More Portraits, More Diaries—Ancestors Again

There are other pieces of the past that I want to include in this record, facts and purported facts that bear on the world I know so imperfectly—the world of the ancestors.

The first has to do with Alexander Henderson, owner of Grove Plantation, of Adam, and of Ike Giddings and his son John. Henderson was a bachelor all his life. My siblings and I own an ambrotype of him in his sixties. It sits on the mantelpiece of the house my father grew up in. I look again and again at his strong, intelligent face, the lips closed firmly in what is almost a smile, the eyes, it seems to me, full of tolerance and pity and understanding. On the back of this picture is written, in my great-aunt's hand, the following:

> Portrait of Alexander C. Henderson
> Grove Plantation, Adams County, Miss.

> A Christian gentleman whose whole life, with a heartful of love, was devoted to his brothers and sis-

ters, their children and grandchildren who gathered yearly in his home to enjoy his royal hospitality. He was a veteran of the War of 1812 and actively engaged in the Battle of New Orleans.

Portrait by Anderson
Artist and photographer
New York City
1858 or 1859

To Richardson Ayres
from
C.M.H.—1942

Richardson Ayres was my father, C.M.H. was his aunt Corinne Henderson. There is no evidence that Henderson (named for his ancestor, the great Scottish divine) was in Adams County when Ike and John were examined. We do not know where he was or what he thought or did.

Nor do we know, although it seems likely, whether Obey and Dick and Adam and Ike and John were among those executed. What I have said about that is either my deduction or Winthrop Jordan's deduction. We simply do not know anything except that they were examined.

The second addition to this record is made up of

entries from the diaries of Dr. Joseph Stratton, who was the Presbyterian minister in Natchez for more than fifty years, beginning in 1843. Here is the text for his ordination sermon: "For they watch for your souls, as those that must give account." (Dr. Stratton, incidentally, was the grandfather of Caroline, who danced for pennies in the barbershop with my mother.) Here is his diary entry for August 9, 1857: "Preached at Forest Church in morning and to negroes at Mr. Edwin Bennett's in afternoon." Over the years there are frequent references to preaching to black congregations.

Stratton was active, as were the Henderson men, in the Mississippi chapter of the American Colonization Society, which raised money to return freed slaves to Africa—to Liberia. Today the descendants of these free people face each other in the bloody streets of Monrovia.

Of the three hundred members of Stratton's congregation in 1862, fifty-seven were colored. He cared for their souls. Here is an excerpt from his "Quarter Century Anniversary Discourses" in January 1869:

> Many from this class [the colored] were added to the church; and a faithful walk has demonstrated of some of them at least, that they were neither insincere nor mistaken in professing themselves Christians. I have seen too many instances among them of faith work-

ing by love and purifying the heart, of piety leading
to correctness of life . . . to allow me to doubt that
the grace of the gospel . . . can still, among them as
among others, convert the natural man into a new
creature in Christ.

Over the years Dr. Stratton suffered from bouts of
deep depression, thought much of death, was tempted
to suicide. "My heart seems very dull. I cannot feel anything, and I do not seem to live anywhere," he writes,
and "I am not happy and life does not promise me hap-
piness, and hence I wish to quit life." He accuses himself
of pride, of overweening ambition, of the weakness of
the flesh. I suppose that, like many Calvinists, he was
tormented by reasonless guilt.

Reading his diaries, I could not but be aware of his
unquestioning commitment to the Confederacy. Although he was born in New Jersey and still had relatives
in the North, he does not mention concern for his faraway family during the war years, or question the legit-
imacy of the Confederate cause.

There is only one entry in his diary regarding the
proceedings of the committee of gentlemen of the neighborhood. It is dated September 23, 1861. "A number of
negroes were executed on Sat 20th near Forest Church,
charged with plotting an insurrection. The public mind
has been agitated on the subject during the week."

Finally, there is Alfred Vidal Davis Sr., father of my suicidal grandfather. His wife was born Sarah Surget and one of his grandmothers was a Dunbar. There is no indication in Conner's notes that any of the slaves involved in the "insurrection" belonged to him. During the fall of 1861 Davis was captain commanding the Natchez Rifles, operating in the Army of Kanawha near Sewell Mountain, in western Virginia. I am aware of no reference by him or any of his family to the proceedings of the committee.

But one of his former slaves, John Roy Lynch, came to considerable prominence during Reconstruction, first as a member of the state legislature, then as Mississippi secretary of state, later as a member of the United States Congress. Lynch practiced law in Washington, D.C., and in Chicago, lived into the 1930s and wrote at some length of Davis in his autobiography. Of the Davises he says that "for slave owners they were reasonable, fair, and considerate. Their house servants were very much attached to them." Of himself as a house servant, a lad in his teens, Lynch wrote, "It was my duty, among others, to brush the flies from the table during meal hours."

At the time of the federal occupation of Natchez in 1863, Lynch had been for almost two years a field hand on the Davis plantation, Tacony, in the malarial swamps of Louisiana. As I've written elsewhere, he had been sent there shortly before Mr. Davis and his troop departed for Virginia because (as he stood waving away the flies in the dining room) he had displeased Mrs. Davis by a too clever answer to a question from Mr. Davis.

Like thousands of other slaves on other plantations, when federal troops moved into the area, Lynch walked away from Tacony. He managed to sell a chicken to a Yankee soldier for a dime and used the dime to buy passage across the river in a small boat. He made his way to Dunleith, the Davis home in Natchez, where he hoped to find his mother. But she, along with all the other house servants, had also walked away.

Lynch writes, "My heart almost melted when I saw Mrs. Davis in the kitchen endeavoring to prepare something for herself, husband, and children to eat." Of Davis he writes that

> the visible moisture of his eyes revealed the sadness and sorrow of a broken heart. A few days prior to that time he was not only in opulent circumstances, with money, property, and many slaves at his service, but he was a strong and fortunate factor politically and otherwise in the community in which he lived. His word was law and his personal presence commanded attention, reverence, and respect. Now he found himself without power, without prestige, without slaves, and almost without means. It was a

sad and pitiful picture. Even my own presence brought forcibly to his mind the humiliation to which he was then subjected, for I was no longer obliged to address him or refer to him as "master," but merely as Captain or Mr. Davis. Still my heart went out with some degree of sympathy for him.

When he was a young man, Alfred Sr. experimented with growing grapes in the sandy land of his Gulf Coast property, hoping to open up a winery there, but the climate was not right and the venture was a failure. When I was a child, there was still a grape arbor in my grandmother's yard that bore small, sweet grapes—all that was left of Great-Grandfather Davis's wealth and power. Now, that, too, is gone.

1994: Gold Jr., His Funeral and Afterwards

The funeral was to be held at Morning Star Baptist Church, a country church just a few miles from our farm. I set out for the church with Larry Hutchins, the manager of my brother's small cattle operation. (Hutchins, incidentally, is another name with a two-hundred-year history in the county, and Larry is another black man from whom I had learned nothing about the Plan.) It was a cold January day, rain falling steadily. We were to meet my son at the church. A member of the state legislature, he had political business in Jackson and would have to hurry to get home in time for the funeral. I was anxious—worried that driving too fast in this weather he might meet with an accident—and I was relieved when he drove up, safe, just after Larry and me. Cars were parked all along the shoulder of the blacktop road and the church was already almost full. The three of us found seats together toward the back. My son and Larry knew many of the people there and nodded to acquaintances, but I knew no one except for two white men seated across the aisle from us, the county chancery clerk and his brother, longtime Democrats and political colleagues of Gold's. There was no other white person present—no one from the Democratic Executive Committee on which he had served, not one white person who taught with Gold's wife, no one from among the whites he had worked with in the old union at Armstrong Rubber Company, not even anyone from the store down the road from his house where he had traded for years.

As we came in, we were handed printed programs for the service—folded leaflets—as is customary in many black churches. Gold's photograph was on the front—that strong face: high cheekbones, stern mouth, and broad forehead. He stared out at us with dark, accusing eyes.

The funeral was an unusual one: The service was to be conducted by a rabbi. As we learned from the rabbi's remarks, Gold had left his church, the Baptist church in which he was raised and where his funeral was being held, and joined the House of Israel. For some time he had been driving eighty miles to Vicksburg to attend Sabbath services there. He had a new name. He was Brother Dan, a black Jew. Now the rabbi and a minyan had come down for his burial. They came in behind the coffin, ten black men wearing prayer shawls and yarmulkes, and they conducted the service, reading passages from the Old Testament, and speaking in praise of their brother. Philip West spoke for Gold, too—Philip West, in whose house Gold had stood watch many a night during the Civil Rights years when West was president of the local NAACP. There were a few special people, he said, and Gold was one of them. My son spoke and told how he had gone to Gold for guidance and advice when he had first gone into politics. My son said that what he knew about Gold, what he counted on, was that in the face of whatever difficulty, he always did the right thing.

After the service, we drove the eight or so miles into Natchez and stood by while he was buried in the National Cemetery, graveyard for so many thousands of Union soldiers killed in the western campaigns of the Civil War. When I was a child, I remember, black people used to gather from all around the county on Memorial Day and march there to lay wreaths on the graves of black soldiers. Perhaps they still do.

Of course, any serviceman has the right to be buried there, and Gold had served his time in the army.

What else? I began a new search—this time asking what it had meant, that funeral, what had happened in his life that had brought him in his old age to the House of Israel. I spoke with Philip West and others of his friends, people who had worked with him at Armstrong or in the movement. Gold was always one who despised hypocrits, Philip said. He looked for people to be what they said they were. And "He said he would stick with me until I died. And he did. He stayed with me all through the dangers—during registration, the boycott, in the union, in the schools—all the way." In those days, the Civil Rights days, another said, it was dangerous even to belong to the NAACP. One friend told me that when they passed the Civil Rights laws and you couldn't have water fountains marked COLORED at Armstrong any more, the white workers would bring their own water rather than share a fountain with the blacks.

"Do they still do that?" I asked.

"No, no, I suppose they've forgotten all about that," he said.

Another called the names of black churches burned in the county: Pilgrim Rest, Duck Pond, Jerusalem. But when I asked about Gold's last years, they shook their heads. "He'd had that stroke, you know," they said. "And then, nursing his mama and daddy and Lawrence. He was under a strain." But the House of Israel? No one wanted to speak to me of that. No one, I believe, wanted to think about it.

I made an appointment with his wife and went back to his little house on Second Creek and talked with her. I asked if she had gone with him to the services in Vicksburg and she said she had not. It was clear to me that she did not want to talk about the House of Israel. She spoke, though, of other things about Gold.

He'd read the newspaper like it was a textbook, she said. Every day, cover to cover. Everybody came to him to find out what was happening—in the legislature, in the union, in the welfare department, in the party. He would always know. Injustice went all over him, she said. That was in the old days.

But no, she did not know why he'd gone into the House of Israel. He was disheartened, she said. Folks didn't come by much. And, no, again, she had not gone to that church with him.

Day after day, toward the last, she said, he'd sit at the breakfast table by the window that looked out across Liberty Road. Across the road from his house is the county barn, the location of his precinct's voting place. Behind the barn rise acres and acres of deep green pines.

"He'd just sit there, quiet, staring out the window. He'd never say a word," she said.

Just now and then, if she'd ask him, "Gold, how are you? Gold, are you all right?" he'd say, "All right." And sometimes he'd shake his head and say, "The people don't want nothing. They don't want nothing."

The people had stopped caring about their rights? About the cause? About justice? The people no longer cared enough to risk their lives, as they had in the old days? Was he looking beyond the county barn into the deep green forest, thinking that his witness, his life, had gone for nothing?

1996: More Ancestors

Later I listened to weekly broadcasts of a Bible study program conducted by Brother Divine of the House of Israel. He read to us verses from Genesis concerning the twins Jacob and Esau and how they strove together in their mother's belly and how Esau sold his birthright to Jacob for a mess of pottage and how later Jacob by trickery received the blessing from their father that should have gone to Esau as the elder, and how Jacob thus became the progenitor of the Chosen People, the Israelites. Esau was a red and hairy man, he told us, and Jacob was a smooth man. He went on to explain to us that the black people of the world, the smooth men, were descended from Jacob, and the white people from Esau. Our hairy brother, he said, can't forget that we outsmarted him. It is clear, he said, that black people are truly the Chosen People, the descendants of Abraham and Isaac, and of Jacob who bought the birthright and received the blessing. White people are the descendants of Esau. For a long time, he said, black people feared white people, just as Jacob on his return to the home he had left years before feared that Esau might slay him; also, he said, sometimes black people fell away from their faith and did evil in the sight of the Lord. They were enslaved in Egypt and they suffered greatly in the wilderness. But Jacob and Esau were reconciled and Jacob's children, the Children of Israel, escaped from Egypt and from the wilderness and multiplied and prospered. We have much to do as a people, Brother Divine said. And, we've got to love one another. And, the world will be free when the Negro is free.

Of course there are many other things to be said, to be taken into account.

Gold became Brother Dan when he joined the House of Israel. He took his name from Dan, the son of Jacob and his wife Rachel's handmaiden, Bilhah. Afterwards Rachel said, "God hath judged me and hath also given me a son." In Genesis, when Jacob is dying, Dan, like his brothers, receives his own special blessing from his father.

"Dan shall judge his people," Jacob said. "Dan shall be a serpent by the way, an adder in the path, that biteth the horse heels, so that his rider shall fall backward."

This is the message Gold left us.

And Obey's message? None, for he is silent. Obey is silent. Bill Postlethwaite, Orange, Dick . . . They are all silent.

My cousin Liza Conner Martin died not many months after Kathie and I called on her. But we still have, lying in the archives at LSU, her grandfather Lemuel Conner's notes, his record of the proceedings conducted by the "gentlemen of the neighborhood," the four handwritten pages that lay so long in the drawer of the nightstand in the Conner bedroom where Liza's mother and father slept.

Four pages with, at the end, that string, that dreadful string of names:

Obey, Obey, Obey, John O. Fenall, Obey, Obey, Obey, Obey, Obey, Obey, Obey, Obey.
                      end

                    Harry Scott
                    George
                                        " " " " " " " " " " " " " "

Alfred

                    Dick